Dedication

"Blessed are the peacemakers"

This book is dedicated to the loving memory of our four
very young, dedicated and caring RCMP Constables,
Peter Schiemann age 25, Lionide Johnston age 34,
Anthony Gordon age 28, and Brock Myrol age 29,
who tragically and very sadly lost their lives in
the line of duty on March 3, 2005.

These four young men did the right thing and it is time
for Canadians to also do the right thing in their honour.

"An ounce of prevention is worth a pound of cure"

How we so desperately needed that one single solitary
ounce of prevention before that day, and how one single
moment in time had the ability to place a dark cloud of
despair, that will forever hang over Alberta. It is up to us
now, in a country that we're so proud of and love very
much, to ensure that the light they brought into
everyone's life continues to shine as brightly as their
futures should have been.

The Lone Ranger's Creed

I believe that to have a friend, a man must be one.

That all men are created equal and that everyone has

within himself the power to make this a better world.

That God put the firewood there but that every

man must gather it and light it himself.

In being prepared physically, mentally and morally

to fight when necessary for that which is right.

That a man should make the most of what equipment

he has. That 'this government, of the people,

by the people and for the people' shall live always.

That men should live by the rule of what is

best for the greatest number. That sooner or

later...somewhere...we must settle with the world

and make payment for what we have taken.

That all things change but truth,

and that truth alone, lives on forever.

In my creator, my country, my fellow man.

For Brock

"Hi-ho Silver! Away!"

Acknowledgements

To my son Chris who always seems to somehow quietly share my pain with every tragic event that life lays in our path. For offering your thoughts, opinions and ideas in order to offer a different perspective – to provide me with the opportunity to think from the other side. Sometimes you think I'm not listening – but I always hear everything you say. Thank you for your love, support and understanding.

To Wayne for the love, understanding and endless support when I made the decision to write the book. For your patience with all of the countless hours I spent locked in the den, morning, afternoon, and late into the night every weekend in my efforts to try and make a difference. Thank you for having the faith and confidence in me to know, that I would finish what I started.

To my mother – for everything you do and everything you are. To the person who never stops giving or offering her support, love and understanding. Thank you for sharing my pain and grief. Thank you for always being there.

To Charlie and Caroline – for the support, friendship, family, trust, and honesty. Thank you for allowing me to be reclusive, to invade your privacy, and come up for air when I needed to. To Carol – thank you for participating in the journey, I couldn't have done it without you.

To Dixie – Thank you Reiki Master, for lifting my spirits and kicking me in the behind when it needed kicking – thank you for your love, support, understanding, and words of wisdom. Thanks for the treatments Dixie.

To 4th Floor Press, Inc. – Thank you Johanna for your wise words of advice, guidance, encouragement and support. Most of all, thank you for your endless sense of humour. Anne, thank you for all the support and encouragement, and for always being available to take care of whatever needed taking care of – you're a gem. Wendy – thank you for your hard work, praise and encouragement – it made all the hours of late-night editing not seem quite so overwhelming. You're a great teacher and I have learned a lot. Thank you Wendy.

Foreward

I am no different than you or any other Canadian. I work forty hours a week, spend time with family and have raised my son alone since he was nine months old. He's twenty now and given me much to be proud of. Like any other family, we've been through some very difficult times, but life is like that – you get through it and take each day as it comes.

We are very blessed and fortunate to live in a country as great as Canada. We do our best to help the less fortunate, to be there when needed, and like most of you, expect nothing in return. I wrote this book because I believe that most Canadians have very common goals: successful careers, happy children, better and brighter futures. These commonalities have, on many occasions, united Canadians to overcome troubled times.

When four RCMP officers were murdered in Mayerthorpe, Alberta, something very authentic and tangible started to move the bulk of this nation in a way that made me very proud. For a while at least, we remembered some really important things that are so easily forgotten. I don't want us to forget that sense of unity – it clearly reminded me of what I always believed the people of Canada are made of.

In the last chapter of this book you'll find both a post office box number and an e-mail address. I welcome every Canadian to step forward and be heard. Every letter and e-mail will support the crucial changes required to begin repairing our crumbling justice system. I also implore every Canadian to send a letter or e-mail demanding that our government immediately address the severe lack of funding for police officers to fight the war on crime in Canada. If you just want to send in your comments, please fire away.

You have my solemn promise that I will ensure your letters are carefully read, sorted, compiled, organized and delivered directly to Parliament Hill. For anyone who wishes to send letters directly to our government, you will also find the names and addresses of The Prime Minister of Canada, the Premiers of every province and the Deputy Prime Minister and Minister of Pubic Safety and Emergency Preparedness.

A percentage of the proceeds from the sale of every copy of The Last Post will be donated to the memorial fund that was established for the families of the four RCMP members who lost their lives. God bless them all.

"Ten people who speak make more noise

than ten thousand who are silent."

Napoleon Bonaparte

Chapter 1 – The Tragedy

"Freedom and duty always go hand in hand,

and if the free do not accept the duty of social

responsibility they will not long remain free."

John Foster Dulles

"Nothing is too small to know,

and nothing is too big to attempt."

Cornelius Van Horne

Wednesday, March 2, 2005, two Edmonton-area bailiffs drove out to the farm of forty-six-year-old James Roszko. They were to execute a civil order to repossess a truck that Roszko had in his possession. The farm was located near the village of Rochfort Bridge, approximately 123 kilometers northwest of Edmonton, Alberta. The bailiffs, while en route to the property, requested assistance from the Mayerthorpe RCMP for the purpose of "keeping the peace."

At the farm, a locked gate prevented the bailiffs from going any further. They sounded their horn in an attempt to get Roszko's attention and were promptly confronted by a man approaching them from a Quonset (a rounded steel storage facility). He was shouting obscenities and demanding they get off his property. The bailiffs identified the man as James Roszko. They did not leave the gate. Roszko then released two guard dogs into the yard and proceeded to jump into a white pickup truck, crash through a fence and disappear from the premises heading north. The time was about 3:20 p.m.

Four Mayerthorpe RCMP officers were on their way to the scene. While en route, they were quickly briefed on the situation, and shortly thereafter a group on horseback flagged them down and reported being spooked by a lone male driving erratically in a white truck. They arrived at the scene at approximately 5:30 p.m. The time, location and description were consistent with Roszko's earlier departure from the property.

The bailiffs were unsure if the white truck Roszko was driving when he left the property was the one contained in the seizure notice. Once the RCMP arrived, the bailiffs acted on their Order and proceeded onto the property to search the premises for the truck in question. They cut the lock off the gate, drove to the Quonset and went inside. The dogs had been sedated in the yard as they investigated further. Inside the Quonset, the bailiffs found what appeared to be stolen vehicles in the process of being dismantled, as well as auto parts from a number of different vehicles.

The pungent smell of marijuana was also present inside the Quonset. Upon further investigation, they found a marijuana grow operation with hundreds of plants. Additional support from the Mayerthorpe and Whitecourt RCMP detachments was dispatched to secure the scene while the proper search warrant was processed.

After taping a seizure notice to Roszko's residence, the bailiffs left the farm at approximately 6:30 p.m. The grow operation was investigated later that evening by the Edmonton Police Service "Green Team" after receiving the search warrant. Six additional officers were in attendance to assist throughout the night. The stolen property investigation was scheduled to begin the following morning, March 3, in order to allow the RCMP Auto Theft Unit to conduct their investigation under daylight conditions.

RCMP patrols were made throughout the area in an attempt to locate James Roszko or his truck. They were unable to locate either.

On the morning of March 3, at approximately 3:45 a.m., two officers, Constable Anthony Gordon from the Whitecourt RCMP detachment and Constable Lionide Johnston from the Mayerthorpe RCMP detachment, were assigned to secure the property at the farm. Regular radio contact was made with the members on the property throughout the night. At approximately 4:00 a.m., the Green Team departed the property after having seized approximately 280 marijuana plants. The members at the scene confirmed to their detachment that Roszko had not been sighted during their shift.

Hours later, at approximately 9:00 a.m., two other officers arrived at the Roszko farm. One officer, Constable

Peter Schiemann from the Mayerthorpe detachment, was on duty but dressed in plain clothes at the time. Constable Schiemann was on his way to Edmonton to purchase work-related supplies and was present at the farm only to drop off another member of the Mayerthorpe detachment, Constable Brock Myrol. The RCMP did not, at this time, know where James Roszko was.

Two armed, plain-clothes officers from the RCMP's Edmonton Auto Theft Unit arrived approximately fifteen minutes later. They exited their police vehicle to begin prepping their equipment and noticed all four officers walking east along the south side of the Quonset, which they entered into a moment later. Within seconds, the auto theft officers heard the chilling crack and resounding echoes of rapid gunfire from inside the Quonset.

A man later identified as James Roszko exited the structure and began firing one of his weapons at the auto theft team, hitting a parked police cruiser. Roszko had three clearly visible weapons on his person at the time of the shooting: a Heckler and Koch .308 with a 20-round detachable magazine, a 9mm semi-automatic pistol tucked into his waistband and a long-barreled gun slung over his shoulder. These weapons were identified as such at a later date and time.

When the Auto Theft Unit officers returned fire, Roszko retreated into the Quonset. The call for back-up was placed immediately and the Edmonton Emergency Response Team was deployed, including the Explosive Disposal Unit, Police Service Dog, Edmonton Police Service's Air One, Stars Air Ambulance and the Red Deer Emergency Response Team. After back-up units arrived, more than four hours had passed since the four officers entered the Quonset. Shortly after 2:15 p.m., a tactical team stormed the Quonset to confirm their worst fears.

There on the dark and dirty floor of the building lay five blood-soaked bodies: four fellow officers and their cold-blooded murderer, James Roszko. It appeared that Roszko's fatal gunshot wound was self-inflicted.

Roszko, at some point in time, had sneaked back onto the property without anyone's knowledge. Laying in wait, Roszko ambushed the four young officers and shot them down in cold blood with a Heckler & Koch, model 91, .308 semi/fully-automatic assault rifle – a weapon that is specially made for combat and illegal in Canada. The assault rifle was also equipped with a flash suppressor (a device attached to a rifle to reduce the brilliant muzzle flash that occurs upon firing) and a telescopic lens (to magnify targets in sight).

Calgary, Alberta – March 3, 2005

I had just walked in the door from a long day at work and was greeted by a ringing telephone. I rushed inside and picked up – it was my friend Marcy. Before I could say anything, she told me to turn on the news.

My stomach instantly turned. What was wrong? Marcy didn't say anything else until I found the channel I was looking for. I turned up the volume and stared. A reporter was relaying the facts about what had taken place earlier that morning. Four Royal Canadian Mounted Police officers had been ambushed and gunned down in a Quonset at a rural Alberta farm just outside of Edmonton.

Reality hit me hard and fast. Marcy knew that I have close family friends near Edmonton, and one of them happens to be an RCMP officer. I said goodbye to Marcy and dialed my friends, praying that everything was okay. When Steve picked up, my heartbeat started to slow down as relief washed over me. He was okay.

Later that evening, as I continued to watch every news program I could, I began to cry. It just kind of happened. I suspect that many Canadians did exactly the same. My anger soon replaced my tears. I tried to understand how on earth something like this could have happened here in Alberta. It was a sleepless night.

My alarm went off at six o'clock the following morning. Groggy and sleep-deprived, I made coffee and turned on the radio to catch the six-thirty news update. I heard the names of the four murdered RCMP officers. One name hit me like a ton of bricks: Constable Brock Myrol. The name echoed through my brain over and over again.

My hand flew to my mouth and I let out a garbled scream. As the tears began, I tried to choke back the shock that reverberated through my entire body. I ran for the phone and called my mother. She knew instantly that I had already heard. She was sitting at home deciding how on earth she was going to tell me about Brock.

I have known the Myrol family for the past twenty-two years. They were always there for my family, during some of the most difficult and trying times of our lives. I had watched Brock and his sister, Kali, grow up, for the most part. It was a number of months ago that I had spoken with Colleen and she told me the wonderful news: Brock was going to be an RCMP officer and was in Regina at the training academy depot.

A few minutes later, after I composed myself somewhat, I picked up the phone and called the Myrols. It was by far the most difficult thing I've ever done in my life. I could not imagine what their life was like at that moment. After a short conversation with Colleen and her daughter, I filled up the car, grabbed two cups of coffee and drove to Red Deer, crying most of the way. I stopped about one block away from the Myrol home. There were reporters and cameras everywhere. I cautiously avoided them, shooting dirty looks in their direction, and walked up to the house and rang the doorbell.

Later on that morning, I asked Colleen if there was anything I could do for them. She looked directly at me and, without missing a beat, said, "Yes. You can write to our politicians and government demanding change." It wasn't quite what I expected, but knowing Colleen, I wasn't surprised. I took Colleen very seriously and knew in my heart that she meant every single word she said.

That morning, Colleen, arm in arm with her daughter, slowly walked down the front steps and stood quietly for a moment in front of the throng of reporters and cameras. She had something to say, something that she needed the world to hear and understand:

> The family of Brock Myrol is deeply saddened by the sudden and tragic loss of Brock. However, it is time that our government takes a stand on evil. The man who murdered our son and brother was a person who was deeply disturbed and ill.
>
> It is our duty as Canadians to stop and rethink how we are raising our children. It is time to teach honour in our country. Brock knew that. It is time to care for our fellow man. Brock knew that. It is time to end the violence and stop the bullying on the play ground so our children won't commit suicide. Brock knew that. It is time as parents, whether a single or a two-parent family, to raise our children with honour for a country where a man's word is his bond. Brock knew that.
>
> It is time to take our liberal-minded attitude to task. Prime Minister Paul Martin, we depend on you and expect you to change the laws and give the courts real power. Give the police real power. Take

the power from the Supreme Court and give it back to the House of Commons.

We are a good country. Brock knew that. He loved the RCMP and all it stood for. Our country is hurting. We have lost four dedicated citizens who were willing to do something about it.

Children who are raised with hopes, dreams and goals and not in houses filled with drugs and violence will be better people. Brock knew that. Canadians are loving, caring people, Brock knew that and dedicated his life to preserving that tradition.

From the Myrol family to the families of the other constables that are dealing with their extreme and eternal loss, we are sorry. We share and feel your pain. God bless you all.

That was, by far, the most powerful and honest statement I had heard in a very long time. Her words, I could only hope and pray, would not be forgotten any time soon.

By the time I arrived home in Calgary, I knew what I needed to do. I felt it was my duty, both as a citizen and as Colleen's friend, to effect some change in this country. I wanted to ask every Canadian to help with creating this change. I silently made a promise that day to Colleen, Keith and Kali. I kept that promise – I wrote this book.

The deep sorrow of this unthinkable horror has taken its toll on Canadians and people alike across the globe. Our compassion, grief and emotion became a tidal wave of love, support and understanding because we felt their pain together. As a country, we mourned together. This tragedy cannot be forgotten; these young men cannot and should not die in vain.

Constable Lionide Nicholas Johnston, 32

Leo, as he was known by almost everyone, was born just nine minutes before his twin brother, Lee, in Lac La Biche, Alberta. The two boys were as close as you would expect twins to be, and their relationship was a reflection of their amiable personalities. Leo's parents, brother and sister describe him as incredibly courageous, determined and driven.

Lee shared many wonderful and touching memories at his brother's service on March 11, 2005. He spoke about how Leo was the most important person in his life. They had nicknames for each other that came from watching too many episodes of "The Simpsons": Leo was "Beaner" and Lee was "Boy." He also spoke with great pride about how his brother had the ability to overcome every obstacle that was placed in his path – Leo knew what it meant to be a fighter and what it took to be a warrior. He remembered that Leo's goofy smile and uncontrollable giggle had often kept him out of trouble. Friends and acquaintances said Leo was fearless, kind, well liked, full of life – he lived life on the edge and didn't want it to pass him by.

In 1997, just one week before Lee was scheduled to graduate from the RCMP training depot, Leo was critically injured in a motorcycle crash while racing in Calgary. Both brothers loved the sport. After a lengthy recuperation and recovery, what some people had called miraculous, Leo made a decision to join the RCMP as well. He graduated from training on April 17, 2001, one of his proudest achievements. An expert marksman with a perfect score on his pistol qualification, he wore a special badge on his uniform to signify his accomplishment. Leo was posted to the small community of Mayerthorpe, Alberta.

Leo was married for less than four months when he was killed. In a public statement, his wife, Kelly, stated that once in a lifetime you meet your soul mate, someone who completes you as a person. Leo was her soul mate. She said he was the kind of man who took an innocent and almost child-like pleasure in every moment life had to offer – he gave her every reason to look forward to the next. He deserved to come home that night. He deserved to live.

Constable Anthony Fitzgerald Orion Gordon, 28

Anthony was born in Edmonton, Alberta, with a life-long dream of becoming a Mountie. It was a decision he made at six years old, after an RCMP officer visited his first-grade class. As time passed by and after much hard work trying to achieve that goal, he succeeded and his dream became a reality. Anthony graduated with much pride from the RCMP Depot in Regina, Saskatchewan on October 15, 2002. He was posted to the community of Whitecourt, Alberta.

Anthony was known as the kind of guy who put everyone at ease. He loved to play sports and camp. His wife, Kim, and young son were the most important people in his life. They always had first consideration in his world. He was also going to be a father again for the second time. He was looking forward to the new baby and to growing old with Kim and his children around him.

Anthony was a friendly, gentle giant of a man with a big smile and a bigger heart. He loved to laugh and he loved his family and friends. He was like a "Seinfeld" episode, where the jokes were about nothing but you always found yourself laughing anyway.

He was a husband, a father, a son, a friend and a colleague – and he was best at all of those things. Anthony cared deeply about being an RCMP officer. He was proud of being a part of the family of men and women who maintained the right.

Constable Brock Warren Myrol, 29

Brock was born in Outlook, Saskatchewan, a small community not far from Saskatoon. It was not surprising that Brock had more close friends than most people – he was like a magnet drawing people to him. His spirited nature and endless zest for life landed him in exotic destinations like Africa and Australia.

Brock's close-knit family moved to Red Deer, Alberta, in 1983. As a little boy, Brock loved the Lone Ranger; he wanted to grow up and be just like him. You could often hear his delighted boyish voice singing "Hi-ho, Silver! Away!" He cheered on the good guys with the zealous exuberance reserved for small children.

Brock had a talent for singing, song writing and guitar playing. He also had an innate capability for the martial arts, where he attained a black belt. He worked as a security officer and it was ultimately that which finally led to his decision to become a Mountie.

Brock became engaged to Anjila, the love of his life, in 2004, and graduated from the training depot in Regina on February 7, 2005. He was chosen their class valedictorian and was humbled by the honour. Posted to Mayerthorpe as the newest member of the detachment, he started his first shift on Valentine's Day. He wanted to make a difference and be a part of the solution. An acquaintance of Brock's had commented that he could have been the poster boy for the Mounties – he was exactly what you'd want to see.

His family said he always set the bar and jumped over it. His honesty, integrity and passion for life were remark-able and he was always on the side of "right." He was a man of honour, dignity and respect. In Colleen Myrol's words, Brock was good for your soul.

Constable Peter Christopher Schiemann, 25

Peter was born in Petrolia, Ontario, the son of a Lutheran Minister and a school teacher. He was the middle child of three with one older brother and a younger sister. Their family eventually found themselves settled in the community of Stony Plain, Alberta. It was said that Peter was dedicated to the three most important things in his life: his family, his faith and the law.

One of Peter's teachers called him the salt of the earth, a man who loved God and loved people. He was kind and generous, and went out of his way to help people. Many close family friends were members of law enforcement, and Peter's brother said it was something he wanted to do for a very long time. He chose a career in policing because he felt he was a more one-on-one kind of person in terms of his strengths and abilities.

High school teachers commented that he pursued his goals with decorum and determination. He was a member of the school choir and the curling team. After graduation, he always came back to watch his sister's basketball games. Peter then took on the task of putting himself through university by working part-time jobs and ultimately ended up graduating from the RCMP training academy on November 27, 2000. He was posted to Mayerthorpe to begin his policing career.

Peter was always known as a kind, dedicated and gentle man who wanted nothing more to do than to help others. Peter's father said he gave his life in the service of God and country, and he so wished he could have taken the bullet for him. Peter always told his family that if he died, to bury him with a bag of chips and a flashlight, because it would be dark and he'd get hungry. They did just that.

The Scars Left Behind – James Roszko and The Failure of Our Justice System

In June 2005, three long and difficult months after the tragedy that shocked this nation, James Roszko's autopsy report was finally completed and released. It confirmed that he had died of a self-inflicted gunshot wound close to the heart. Toxicology reports indicated there was no sign of drugs or alcohol in his system, with the exception of an over-the-counter cold medicine. Another fact confirmed by the autopsy report: Roszko had been wounded by two separate bullets fired by RCMP officers that same day. The officer, or officers, that delivered the two wounding gunshots – one in the hand and one in the thigh, was not revealed. At least the coward suffered.

James Roszko does not deserve any civil acknowledgement, and it is not my wish to add to his notoriety. It is, however, imperative that Canadians learn who Roszko was, and how he was rarely (or inadequately) punished. He was a habitual criminal with a lengthy criminal record. He owned guns, terrorized his community and yet was still able to walk the streets a free man. His own father, Bill Roszko, called his son a "wicked devil."

After the shooting, there were a number of reports about how the Mayerthorpe community felt about Roszko. Whenever he spent time in jail, people in that small town felt a certain amount of relief – they went to bed at night feeling a little safer. When he was not in jail, the entire town and community kept a closer eye on their children. They were a little more wary and careful. As the townspeople began to register their shock and anger, they had to admit that it was really no surprise at all. With a fuse like Roszko's, it was only a matter of time before he exploded like a bomb, leaving behind devastating results.

James Roszko had a very lengthy criminal record, cited below, that began almost three decades ago, in 1976 (any criminal charges previous to that time would have been when Roszko was considered a juvenile, or as we know the term today, a young offender. Because of the protection offered today by Canada's legislation regarding youth and their criminal history, that information is not available):

- 1976 – Roszko was charged with property offences including break and enter and possession of stolen property, harassment and ignoring court conditions.
- 1993 – After an altercation with a local school trustee over moving a school bus stop, Roszko was charged with twelve offences, including unlawful confinement, pointing a firearm, assault with a weapon, possession of a weapon dangerous to the public and impersonating a police officer. Of the twelve charges only seven went to trial. He was acquitted on all seven charges.
- 1993 – According to court documents, Roszko was charged with "counseling another person to commit murder" after he offered someone a price of $10,000 to complete the requested task. The charge was dropped after a preliminary hearing where a judge made a ruling that talking about killing someone isn't the same as plotting to kill someone.
- 1993 to 1998 – Mayerthorpe RCMP, armed with search warrants, went out to Roszko's farm on three separate occasions looking for illegal and/or unauthorized weapons. Officers found and seized two weapons during those searches, a shotgun and a 9mm handgun.

- 2000 – In April, Roszko was convicted of sexually assaulting a young teenage boy over a seven-year period, marking the first significant crime that he ever spent any time in prison over. He was sentenced to two-and-a-half years.
- 2000 – The courts banned Roszko from owning firearms. Once the court imposes that ban, Alberta's Chief firearms officer would have been notified.
- 2001 – In April. Roszko was charged with five offences in connection with an incident that took place in September, 1999. The charges included aggravated assault, pointing a firearm, and assault with a weapon that stemmed from the use of a twelve-gauge shotgun on two people who were on his property. During the incident, it was alleged that shots were fired and the gun was used to bash one of the individuals. The charges were later dismissed; the Crown had produced no evidence.

The prosecutor's office met with difficulties in rounding up available witnesses to testify because they were all scared to death. One of the last people to testify against Roszko admitted he slept with a knife under his pillow every night, until March 3, when he learned that Roszko was dead.

- 2001 – In December, Roszko was denied parole for his sexual assault conviction. He was, however, granted "statutory release," which allowed him to serve out the final one-third of his sentence under supervision in the community and under conditions of release similar to those imposed on offenders released on full parole. In other words, even though he was denied parole, he was released anyway.
- 2001 – In June, just six months after his statutory release from prison, Roszko was arrested for refusing

to cooperate with his parole officer. Correctional Service of Canada told a parole board panel that this refusal made assessing his risk to the community "impossible." Roszko was temporarily sent back to prison for his lack of cooperation.

- 2002 – In August, the parole board was finished with him. His two-and-a-half year sentence was expiring. They simply washed their hands and set him free to roam the countryside again.
- 2004 – In August, Roszko was charged with mischief when spike belts were used to discourage visitors from entering his property. Police were called out to the property when spike belts reportedly disabled vehicles that belonged to provincial census takers.

It is abundantly clear that Roszko was a threat to the community. Do we really have to ask why spike belts were used on his property? What was he trying to hide that needed to be so intensely guarded and protected? There was also talk of "booby traps" that lined two fences around the perimeter of the property. The "NO TRES-PASSING" signs were everywhere.

I hardly believe that the 280 marijuana plants that RCMP located and seized inside the Quonset were for his own personal use. Which potential gang of organized criminals was he working with?

National Parole Board documents indicated a number of red flags with Roszko. He disdained authority, a behaviour he displayed from the time he was a teenager. While in prison, a facilitator concluded that he was unable to recognize his difficulty managing his emotions. Also stated in these documents were the primary factors that should have been addressed in terms of his criminal history: anger, sexual offending behaviour (inappropriate) and attitude. There was also Roszko's blatant refusal to cooperate with his parole officer that, as Correctional

Service Canada said, made assessing his risk to the community "impossible."

Albertans do not want this province to go down in history as the site of a police shooting. It has caused us more pain than we were willing to bear. Albertans would much prefer that this tragedy go down in history as a disastrous loss of life that caused the most changes in the history of Canada, politically and judicially.

The questions as to how and why this tragedy occurred are here for all to see. Only some of them have been answered, and that is not acceptable. Canadians' initial gut reaction was to blame someone for this loss and devastation, and the need to hold someone responsible was great. The RCMP immediately shouldered the brunt of the accusations and criticism. Truth be told, the RCMP are not responsible. They are trying desperately to do their jobs with the meagre resources that are available to them, and their complaints have gone unheard. They are losing the war against crime and violence, and the Canadian public has become collateral damage.

Some statistics report a lower crime rate in Canada, while others report an increase in organized crime. Contradictions abound, but the big picture tells us that Canada has a problem with crime, and punishment. Should we wait for the next round of statistics, or should we start taking some measures to ensure a positive outcome?

At election time, go out and cast your ballots. The federal government needs to listen to our concerns and make new inroads for our safety. Their complacency on this issue is a crime itself. If we don't voice our concerns about out failing justice system and the lack of policing and resources, then we have no right to complain about the wrongs in this country. I believe it's not only for what we do that we are held responsible, but also for what we do not do.

Canada is a peaceful nation, but in order to keep it that way, we need to send a very clear message to the criminals who reside here. Our approach needs to be united, visible, vocal and decisive. Our willingness to unite and demand changes to and from our government, legislation, justice system and more importantly, in our attitudes, will make Canada a stronger, and safer, country. This is everyone's problem. We cannot allow another James Roszko to roam the streets, free to terrorize, assault and kill at will. We do not have to accept this tragedy and walk away.

Hundreds of people across the country sent messages of condolences and wrote to their local newspaper. During the Queen of England's visit, she took time out of her schedule to meet with the families of Peter, Brock, Leo and Anthony. Prime Minister Paul Martin called each of the families, offered his condolences and attended the memorial service that was covered on national television. I know first-hand that the families were appreciative of every gesture, every kind word. I also know that the demand for change has not lessened any since that time. Mr. Martin shouldn't have stopped there, but apparently he did.

The next ten chapters will serve to educate Canadians on every angle that relates to the Mayerthorpe tragedy. Realities and truths will be addressed and discussed with the goal of presenting the powerful knowledge of what the research had to say. I will attempt to demystify the judicial system, its sentencing practices, its judges, its prison system; to criticize and question Canada's politicians and policies; to go inside the RCMP and law enforcement, describe what they're up against and how it impacts society as well as their personal lives; and to analyze the growing problem of Canada's young offenders.

Prepare yourself. Some outrageous stuff is happening in your own backyard.

Chapter 2 – The RCMP and Law Enforcement

"A hero is someone who understands the

responsibility that comes with his freedom."

Bob Dylan

"United we stand, divided we fall."

Aesop

Clancy of the Mounted Police

In the little Crimson Manual
it's written plain and clear

That who would wear the scarlet coat
shall say good-bye to fear;

Shall be a guardian of the right,
a sleuth-hound of the trail –

In the little Crimson Manual
there's no such word as "fail" –

Shall follow on though heavens fall,
or hell's top-turrets freeze,

Half round the world, if need there be,
on bleeding hands and knees.

It's duty, duty, first and last,
the Crimson Manual saith;

The Scarlet Rider makes reply:
"It's duty-to the death."

And so they sweep the solitudes,
free men from all the earth;

And so they sentinel the woods,
the wilds that know their worth;

And so they scour the startled plains
and mock at hurt and pain,

And read their Crimson Manual,
and find their duty plain.

Knights of the lists of unrenown,
born of the frontier's need,

Disdainful of the spoken word,
exultant in the deed;

Unconscious heroes of the waste,
proud players of the game,

Props of the power behind the throne,
upholders of the name:

For thus the Great White Chief hath said,
"In all my lands be peace",

And to maintain his word he gave his
West the Scarlet Police.

By Robert William Service of the Mounted Police

In Regina, Saskatchewan, at the RCMP Chapel, there stands a haunting symbol: a cenotaph honouring 209 RCMP members who have fallen in the line of duty over the last 130 years. Within hours of the senseless tragedy outside of Mayerthorpe, four red roses were placed as a symbol of Canada's loss at the base of the Memorial Wall Plaque. Their names have now been carefully inscribed as a reminder of their sacrifice.

A letter of condolence sent to the RCMP from a woman living in Blairmore, Alberta, eloquently details the reality that police and their families deal with everyday:

I waited by the phone on Thursday and prayed for it to ring. I also prayed the doorbell would not. You see, I am an RCMP member's wife, and my husband was away for weeks on duty without any way for me to reach him, nor could he reach me. All I heard initially on the news was that four RCMP officers were killed in Alberta and so began our wait. My husband always told me, if anything bad happens, they will come to the door. The phone is good, the doorbell is not. How do we express our condolences to the families of these fallen heroes for whom we have a special bond? All of us wives wait by our phones and pray, but with relief comes guilt. We were separated by tragedy this time, but that means that another member's family was not, and there is little comfort in that.

The murder of these four officers is the worst tragedy in recent Canadian history. If you happen to know someone in law enforcement, then you're probably aware of one thing for sure: This senseless and preventable act does not weaken the resolve of law enforcement; it strengthens it with a force so powerful that it should not be reckoned with or taken lightly. It is our duty as citizens to do everything we can to ensure that the power of this force withstands even the most evil and vile criminals. Grief and solidarity know no jurisdiction.

We need police and RCMP, and obviously a lot more of them. I believe it takes a very special and dedicated person to make a decision of this nature, one fraught with personal sacrifice. If we didn't have people like this, who would protect us? They deal with all of the ugliness in the world so the rest of us don't have to. They are an integral part of society and should not be taken for granted. It seems, though, Canada's federal government is doing just that.

There is a gross lack of funding for officers working on the front lines. The RCMP and other law enforcement agencies have, over the past number of years, admitted that there is a certain degree of complacency on their part, that they have no other choice but to work with what they've been given and make the best of it. Officers must work that much harder and spend more time at their jobs because of the serious lack of financial resources to fight crime and accomplish their goals. There are many things that are out of their power to control.

Frontline RCMP officers have expressed dire concern regarding standard-issue firearms and body armour. Standard-issue body armour basically spreads the concentrated impact of a gunshot over their full area and is intended to reduce the probability of penetration. Corporal Wayne Oakes of the Edmonton RCMP publicly stated on March 5, 2005, that standard-issue body armour isn't heavy enough to stop high-calibre bullets. Professor Doug Perovic, Chairman of the University of Toronto's engineering department, has also publicly stated that "there are new materials [for vests] that might do the job even better, but that would be even more expensive than our already cash-strapped police service want to pay." He added, in response to the Mayerthorpe tragedy, "I don't know exactly what the Mounties' vests were, but if they're standard-issue, that's asking a lot of the material." Officers have requested that trauma plates – capable of preventing bullet/weapon penetration – be issued for their vests. Their requests have been repeatedly denied: too expensive.

Al Koenig, President of the Calgary Police Association, has expressed concern over body armour as well. The vests they use are the same as the RCMP's and cannot stop knives or high calibre rounds of ammunition. His officers have asked for enhanced body armour, which would cost over an estimated $1,000,000. Alberta is the most prosperous province in the country; our provincial government can't possibly expect us to believe that they can't afford this drop in the bucket, and without a tax hike. Look at it this way: There are just over a million people in Calgary-if every citizen contributed one dollar, the Calgary Police Service could have their vests, and potentially their lives. The funds to protect officers can and should be available.

Firearms and vests aren't the only concerns for officers. They are also lacking dashboard cameras and encryption devices (to scramble a criminal's use of a police scanner), as well as too few patrol cars to make response times acceptable and too few officers on night duty. It's been reported that James Roszko owned a police scanner, possibly allowing him to know every move the RCMP made that day. Another shocker: Alberta's RCMP officers actually use second-hand radio equipment. It was outdated the day it was purchased in 1991. Bikers on the highway have better radio equipment than this. Can you imagine an officer placing a call for back-up assistance and his radio transmission dies? It's happened many times and will continue to happen unless we force change.

There is absolutely no excuse for this. During the G-8 Summit, in June 2002, in Kananaskis Country, Alberta, security measures were the finest that Canada had to offer. The security officers here had the best radio equipment and communications systems that money could buy. This begs the question: Why isn't this equipment available to Alberta RCMP officers?

If our police officers are not protected, then neither is society. We should all be concerned about this injustice and be willing to do something about it. Politicians should be ashamed. Perhaps they should be the ones to approach an officer's home, to ring the doorbell and inform the family that their loved one has died in the line of duty.

In 2003, the federal government in Ottawa collected approximately $12.8 million from criminal assets across Canada. Over the past five years, the Calgary Police Service has seen only $332,000 of the $2,000,000 that Ottawa gave the province of Alberta. Calgary police believe they're not receiving their fair share of money generated.

Let's calculate Calgary's fair share based on a per capita basis (population):

Between 1999 and 2003, a span of five years, criminal assets would approximate $50,000,000, based on an average dollar amount of $10,000,000 per year.

$50,000,000 divided by 32,000,000

  (population of Canada) = $1.56 per citizen.

$1.56 multiplied by 1,025,000

  (population of Calgary) = $1,599,000.

In the simplest mathematical terms, the City of Calgary probably should have received approximately $1.6 million over this five-year period. Again, this begs the question: What logical equation did the federal government use to justify its numbers province by province?

Further research into the seizing of criminal assets unearthed a report from *Statistics Canada* that stated for the year 2000/01 (no reports available for 2001/02, 2002/03, 2003/04), forfeiture proceeds totaled $10.7 million. The report also noted that the RCMP Integrated Proceeds of Crime (IPOC, based in Ontario's "O" Division) units impounded assets valued at approximately $23.6 million. Where is all this money going? I'll tell you one thing for certain: Canadian law enforcement frontline officers know where it *isn't* going.

There are other money issues to be considered as well. Check out an RCMP website and you'll see the annual salary an officer can expect. A rookie officer starts his or her career at approximately $39,500 per year. Realistically speaking, how can anyone be expected to put his or her life on the line every day for this kind of remuneration?

Every law enforcement officer would let you know that they're not in it for the money. Most officers feel a profound sense of duty; something that can't be bought. Even so, should they not, at the very least, be provided with more help and support?

Politicians are notorious for denying the requested funds for particular areas of public interest but have readily made millions available in foreign aid to help out other countries around the world. Our government should put its citizens first and be much more concerned with what's happening in their own backyard. When our people are fed, clothed, housed and protected, with enough police officers and resources to patrol this vast country, then outside interests can be met.

Alberta police officers must also deal with working alone much of the time (especially outside of big city centres) and having too few officers (5123 in 2004) for Alberta's population (3.2 million in 2004). The Alberta provincial policing contract has remained the same since 1981 (when the population was 2.1 million). What this essentially means is that the number of officers has not changed in twenty-four years, even though the population of Alberta has drastically increased.

It wasn't until April 1, 2005, when the Alberta provincial government announced that the province would receive one hundred new RCMP officers this year. With the addition of these new officers, and based on a per capita basis, the number changes from one officer per every 655 citizens, to one officer per every 616 citizens – these numbers are unacceptable. Our government needs to accept responsibility for their negligence.

Police work is a dangerous job. Lives may be lost. We all know that. Throughout the history of Canadian law enforcement, which dates back to the early 1800s, approximately 600 law enforcement and RCMP officers have been killed in the line of duty. In the last one hundred years (1905-2005), Canada lost almost 570 officers. Of the 600 deaths, 270 were attributed directly to violent criminal acts by perpetrators, and even more disturbing is that almost 225 of the 270 officers were shot to death. Factor in another fifteen officers killed by drunk drivers, and thirty corrections officers, prison guards and escorts murdered by inmates, and the total is closer to 650. In the last five years alone, thirty-one officers have been killed in the line of duty. It will only escalate unless something is done.

When an RCMP officer dies in the line of duty, his funeral expenses are not paid for. Officers do have life insurance, but that money is supposed to take care of the family that's been left behind. The funeral arrangements are, and always have been, the responsibility of the officer's family. There are, however, certain instances where the RCMP organization will pay for all of the arrangements, but they're few and far between.

On November 25, 2004, during the 38th Parliament, 1st Session (Edited Hansard – Number 032), a discussion took place in the House of Commons regarding this issue. The RCMP requested that the Treasury Board review RCMP funeral and burial benefits, to revise and modernize the policy. Mr. Rob Anders (Calgary West, CPC) commented during the session that the widow of an officer was stuck with a $20,800 bill after losing her husband in the line of duty. Mr. Anders said, "I do not think that is a fair deal," and "These women are the equivalent, in my mind, of Silver Cross Mothers. They have given a great deal to their country." The Honourable Roy Cullen (Parliamentary Secretary to the Minister of Public Safety and Emergency Preparedness, Lib.) responded with, "[the review] is ongoing."

It's bad enough that law enforcement families have to deal with their devastating loss, let alone having to deal with unexpected costs, but it seems that all the government does is review their problems – old habits die hard.

The majority of law enforcement officers are overworked, underpaid and have been for many years. Extra hours are worked attending court and completing mandatory paperwork. The average officer spends about as much time doing community service work as he does working his regular shifts and is not paid for such work. Although that's pretty gracious, remember, it is also expected of them. Officers volunteer to attend meetings, sit as board members on numerous committees, such as Community Safety and Asset Building for Youth, and they also find time to get involved with our children as role models and coaches.

Compounding all of these problems is the "bonus system," where certain individuals are paid bonuses if their detachment stays under budget for the year. Government documents released in June 2005, show that the federal government gave 91 percent of its "senior" public servants a whopping $32 million in performance bonuses in 2004. There were 4430 eligible public servants at the "executive level," and 4016 received very generous bonuses. The Liberal Government refused to disclose how many crown corporation employees were also eligible, or how much they were paid. This money would have put 800 new police officers on the street and paid their salaries for the first year. It would have paid for 50,000 new vests.

A few days after the tragic loss of Constables Schiemann, Myrol, Gordon and Johnston, information about a bonus system for senior members within the RCMP, and whether it actually exists or not, first began circulating. A reporter posed the question to a senior member of the RCMP. It was emphatically denied. I have interviewed many police officers over the past six months and almost all mentioned this bonus system. I believe it exists, and Canadians deserve to know the truth.

There are some very important facts to keep straight. Canadians should know it is not the frontline officers that are involved with these choices or decisions – they are on the street, doing their jobs and protecting the people.

There is, however, a big difference between what is happening with frontline officers and what is happening with some of the senior members of the RCMP. I don't want to insinuate that all higher-ups are unethical. They have tough choices to make; some make the right choices, some don't.

Most senior members have chosen to take the lives and well-being of their officers as a serious priority.

Another very serious problem has been highlighted in a study that was recently commissioned by the Canadian Police Association and the Canadian Association of Chiefs of Police. The report indicated that a relatively high rate of turnover within the Canadian policing community can be expected within the next few years. The study estimates that nearly one in four officers in Canada will be eligible to retire with full pensions by 2006. If this happens, the Canadian police force will be short about another 15,000 officers coast to coast. Not to mention those who will resign and take early retirement.

Our government should be preparing for this by conducting massive recruiting efforts. Will it happen? We all know the Liberal Government has been a little preoccupied lately with covering up and justifying the illicit squandering of taxpayers' money. The generation behind the baby boomers is much smaller, leaving Canadians in a very precarious position. This begs the question: Will there be enough recruits to fill the vacant positions?

According to *Statistics Canada*, Canada has 188 officers per 100,000 population, about 20 percent lower than the U.S. and Australia, and 25 percent lower than England and Wales. During the past decade, most provinces have experienced declines in per capita policing strength.

This problem has been around for many years, but it's starting to catch up with us. The government must take action now, not in the years to come.

The information provided so far is an attempt to bring awareness of the problems, difficulties and realities of a law enforcement profession. However, the information truly comes alive only when delivered by a seasoned officer. I received an e-mail in April 2005 that was being circulated by officers in Alberta. Constable Steve Smith of the Cold Lake, Alberta, RCMP detachment explained to me that he wrote this e-mail out of sorrow, pain and anger after the Mayerthorpe tragedy and sent it to his entire list of family members, friends and other RCMP members. He wanted everyone to better understand what an RCMP officer faces every single day in the line of duty. Steve believes that he owes it to these four officers to speak out on their behalf:

Subject: It Has To Be Said [1]

Things I feel that I must say in light of the recent assassination of four of my brothers. First, I must state that these are my personal views and not necessarily the views of the RCMP or any governments that I serve. Before I start, I would like to qualify myself and my background and training. I have been a very proud member of the RCMP for the past fifteen years, serving in rural Alberta. Prior to my full time engagement in the force, I served as an auxiliary member of the RCMP for seven years in two detachments in British Columbia. I am an experienced and senior member of this force. My duties over and above general investigations and law enforcement include providing ongoing "firearms and use of force options" training to the members of this force.

We all deal with grief and loss differently, and as such, I suppose, is the reason I feel I must write this.

---

[1] *E-mail has been edited for spelling, punctuation and grammar (Ed.).*

Throughout my career I have often wanted to write letters to the editor frustrated with our justice system or inaccurate details published by the media. On many occasions we, as a police force, have been unfairly criticized based on partial truths and limited facts presented by the media or persons of less desirable qualities.

We, as police officers, quietly and professionally accept this as we are restricted (by civil and criminal liabilities, privacy laws, policies and the potential of hampering good investigations) to reveal all the facts to the Canadian public. If the citizens of this great country were provided with all the situational factors when officers are criticized, I'm confident they would support decisions and actions taken.

The loss of the four members last week is gut-wrenchingly sad and a gigantic loss that has produced unbearable grief. This loss meant many things to many people, but it definitely was not a surprise. The citizens of this great country have no idea what police deal with every day and night; no idea at all. On an average day we receive at least two e-mails warning of people who are dangerous to police for various reasons. Many are known to carry knives or guns and are eager to use them if confronted by police.

Unfortunately, with what the *Canadian Charter of Rights and Freedoms* has turned into, police are limited in proactively addressing the risk. In most of these cases, we are unable to act until something bad happens, leaving the public and police officers vulnerable. Police officers deal with violence more often than most people realize and are, in fact, put in very dangerous situations several times a day. Considering this, injury and death of our members is an expected occurrence. Unlike a soldier, we often don't know who the enemy is.

In the near future we will see the media questioning and criticizing police action and policy over this situation. It is very easy in hindsight to provide a course of action, to alter an outcome. Before the bashing starts, I would like to state these facts in expectation of the areas of criticism that I foresee.

First of all, unlike very large municipal police forces, we have very limited manpower to police vast areas. In most cases, we work alone and are forced into situations with little or no backup. The limited resources we have are based on our provincial contract. Despite our efforts to increase our numbers, the province has not provided more members and money, requiring us to work with numbers allocated in the late 1980s. Despite population growth and crime rates, I think we continue to provide an excellent service and have done a damn fine job. It would have been nice to have placed ten or more members on that farm to watch over things; however, those costs and resources are not available to us. The fact that they had two members there shows due diligence to the situation as, many times, I have guarded crime scenes by myself.

I suspect that the members' service level, experience and training will come under attack. I would like to say right now that if someone has the intention of and is planning to kill a police officer, they will most certainly succeed. These four members were assassinated and provided with no warning or opportunity to react. Why would we place a junior member at a crime scene? How else does someone learning any trade or occupation gain experience and develop skills without exposure? As far as training goes, I am proud to advise that the Mounted Police has one of the finest training facilities and curriculum in the world. Our training produces police officers of the highest calibre. If this was not the case, we would not be in such high demand by the United Nations. We are continually called upon for peacekeeping efforts and to rebuild and train police forces around the world. As for national pride, it should be known that the Royal Canadian Mounted Police is the only police force in the world that polices at the municipal, provincial, national and international levels. That has to say something about our training and capabilities. Police officer safety is paramount in our training and re-certification.

I further suspect that our justice system and Charter of Rights and Freedoms will come under attack (or at least debate), as it most certainly should. I would like to state that I am (as are my colleagues) a strong supporter of our Charter. It guarantees our freedom within this wonderful nation. I further believe that the intent of this Charter was based on solid Canadian beliefs and wholesome values. Having said that, I further believe that the legal defence sector has created a billion dollar business around cutting it up and making loopholes. I do not feel that the present day's accepted legal interpretations were intended when it was drafted.

It is ironic that the very law that was created to protect freedoms as citizens has chained and hand-cuffed us. It has forced us, without recourse, to be victims of criminals and non-productive members of our society. I would suggest that common sense, fairness, reasonable and probable, are traits God has granted to most Canadians, yet withheld from some of our political leaders and our law interpreters.

Allowing the Supreme Court of Canada the power to veto proposed laws based on Charter/constitution interpretation, limits our elected officials' power for change. This, in turn, makes our democratic elections very superficial, which is a frightening consideration.

I heard the father of one of the deceased Mounties say, "Something good will come of this loss." I have been able to see two good things: I have seen the Canadian people rally around their police forces with heartfelt condolences, warm acknowledgements and appreciation for the work we do. For this, we thank you. Your thoughts, prayers and kind gestures touched the hearts of everyone in our extended family.

The second is that Canadians are looking at our justice system and, I believe, wanting change. If positive change is made and lives are saved because of it, then these deaths have not been completely without cause.

In closing, I wish to say, despite what the media or any appointed committees disclose about this occurrence, please remember what I have written. There was no fault with the members, policy or the RCMP. The only thing that may have changed this outcome would have been empowerment of police officers to effectively and proactively address this type of risk. The badly needed increased money and manpower may have influenced this, but likely not, as the killer was focused and determined in his actions.

If you feel change is needed (real change) to our justice system, I urge you to do something about it. Flex your democratic muscle and force democratic change. As police officers, we know who the drug dealers, rapists and psychopaths are, but we need the tools to deal with them. The same law that defines their actions as illegal also prevents us from stopping or punishing their actions. We must put proper deterrents in our court system to ensure that the message of poor behaviour is not acceptable. This is our country, and I feel we must provide our police with the power to protect people again. We, as citizens, must also have the confidence that our police officers will not abuse this power.

If you feel change is not necessary, don't feel obligated to do anything. Your police officers will continue to proudly serve Canadians in the professional way we always have, but please understand the limitations restricting us. Most of all, please, when the next officer dies, don't say it was a surprise.

For those of you who read this whole letter, thank you for letting me vent and grieve in this way. Please feel free to pass this on, if you feel it has any merit; if not, hit delete.

Constable S. (Steve) Smith
Cold Lake, Alberta, RCMP Detachment

Law enforcement as a profession is complex and multifaceted. It cannot be summed up with statistics or by the politics that surround it. The human element is what makes law enforcement a respected and inspiring institution. My closest and dearest friend, Louise, is the wife of an RCMP officer. This chapter cannot end without including her family's experience.

Louise has admittedly been put through the wringer over the past twenty-five years. Both she and her husband find it difficult sometimes to talk about his career and its effect on them and their three children. Sometimes a line is drawn in the sand: there are some things that are never discussed. After the Mayerthorpe tragedy, I decided to step over that line. Both of them opened up about the very real and terrifying events they've experienced.

Louise told me about the first couple of years of their marriage. There were a few times when a uniformed officer had walked up the front steps and rang her doorbell. These were some of the most awful moments of her life. She braced herself, expecting the worst: to hear that her husband is dead. There were times when her husband came home, packed a few things and left without telling her where he was going or how long he'd be gone. She wasn't allowed to know; most of the time, she didn't want to know. As time went by, she became accustomed to her husband's expected and unpredictable lifestyle.

There were times when her husband came home from the office and she sensed that something was terribly wrong and questioned him on these occasions. He admitted he would rather keep his mouth shut than tell her what was really going on – he thought he could contain the fear and deal with it alone.

His denial only worked for a while. One day it all fell apart. He had no choice but to sit Louise down and reveal his anxiety. He showed her a photograph. He told her that if she ever saw this man, to grab the kids and run. The criminal in the photograph had threatened physical violence against their family, had bragged about how he knew where they lived, where their children went to school, what Louise looked like. This criminal had also threatened to burn down their house. She had to face this kind of terror because her husband was a police officer trying to do his job.

Worse than this were the times when her husband admitted to being so terrified he couldn't share what he felt, couldn't bring it into their home. It was during these times that he slept with his loaded service revolver in the nightstand beside their bed. He said if he couldn't protect his own family, then who the hell would?

Louise knew about some of these times. She accepted it and dealt with it the best way that she could.

Louise kept her children close to her at all times. She never took her eyes off them, no matter where they were. She never knew what might happen, and the possibilities that nagged at her made her vigilance impenetrable. Louise said she always did her best to never allow the children to see her shaken or upset.

The children had their own crosses to bear. They took a certain amount of punishment and abuse over the years from other kids. "Your dad's a pig, a stupid cop" were familiar refrains. They tolerated the insults as best they could. They knew how lucky they were to have such a great dad.

There are two sides to everything. The life of a law enforcement officer is not a glorious one. It is, for the majority, a life of hard work, dedication, commitment and sacrifice that not only affects them, but also that of their family. These officers are a very special group of people and they want to make a difference, to help others. They accept the personal sacrifice as part of their duty.

The most difficult part of their job comes from knowing that there will be times when tragedy will strike and news of an officer's death in the line of duty will be delivered. This is the time they know the strong and protective arms of their fellow officers across this country will come together to embrace and hold steady the families and friends left behind. These officers will tell you how proud they are to stand together and say, "this is our family."

Chapter 3 – The Politicians and The Powers That Be

"The crisis of Canada today is the combination of economic problems facing us and the increasing impotency of governments that lack either the will or the resources to do much about it. The tragedy of Canada today is that just when we need a country that's pulling together in common cause, we have one that keeps finding new ways to pull itself apart."

Angus Reid

"It is better to keep your mouth shut and appear stupid than to open it and remove all doubt."

Mark Twain

Canada's federal Justice Department has paid only lip service to enforcing stiffer penalties for criminals. It is our government's responsibility and obligation as described in the *Canadian Charter of Rights and Freedoms* to provide the citizens of Canada with the best law enforcement, with enough officers to patrol our streets and countryside and to provide these officers with the best equipment and resources available to do their jobs.

They have failed. There are more important things on their agenda such as decriminalizing marijuana, legalizing prostitution and creating taxpayer slush funds to ensure their continued abuse of power and control over this land at our expense.

We do not have a money problem in Canada – we have a values and priorities problem.

It is time for politicians to get serious about this business and the criminals who reap the rewards after spilling blood on our streets and across the countryside. Constables Schiemann, Myrol, Gordon and Johnston are dead because Roszko was not where he should have been: in prison. What's even sadder and more unbelievable is that there are hundreds more out there just like Roszko living next door to you or sitting in a restaurant at the table next to you. We don't like to think about these things, but it's time we start. Welcome to reality.

Canada's federal government evidently has no system of checks and balances. This country is in desperate need of politicians who believe in what Abraham Lincoln called, a government "of the people, for the people, and by the people."

Immediately following the tragedy in Mayerthorpe, Prime Minister Paul Martin spoke to Canadians and the media on a number of occasions. Here's a reminder of some of what he had to say:

- "With their loss, we are left numb that a single act of hate has affected so many lives, caused so much grief, interrupted so much love."
- "This terrible event is a reminder of the sacrifice and bravery of the men and women who serve in our national police force, and of the dangerous circumstances which they often confront, in order to make Canada a safer place."
- "Canadians are shocked by this brutality and join me in condemning the violent acts that brought about these deaths."
- "On behalf of the Government of Canada, I would like to express my condolences to the families of the officers who were killed as they carried out their duty in enforcing the law and protecting the public."

Mr. Martin's comments appear heartfelt and sincere. But, sadly, they are empty condolences. The public isn't buying it. His presence at the memorial service in Edmonton angered many Canadians, and I was one of them. Colleen Myrol, Constable Brock Myrol's mother, implored Mr. Martin "to change the laws and give the courts real power. Give the police real power. Take the power from the Supreme Court and give it back to the House of Commons."

If Mr. Martin can be believed, he is disgusted by this violent act and reveres the officers who protect this country. Why then is there nothing on his Liberal agenda to address Colleen Myrol's statement? We can't trust this man. It shouldn't surprise anyone to know that his government's deceits, antics and schemes have given its citizens a great many reasons to be suspicious.

Mr. Martin painted himself as a "promise keeper," a statement made on March 5, 2005, while addressing delegates at the Liberal Party's first policy convention in five years. The Prime Minister said, "Yesterday was a very hard day for our nation. For generations, for as long as there has been a Canada, the Mounties have served us, they have protected us, they have kept us safe...and that is why we grieve so deeply when they're lost and that is why we grieve today."

After one minute of silence to honour our lost soldiers and the singing of the national anthem, his speech continued: "It was less than a year ago that we were on the campaign trail. We made commitments to the people of our nation. We offered a plan to help Canadians seize their potential and we have delivered on our word. Time and again, we have sent the same message to Canadians: promises made, promises kept."

He also claimed that *"the Charter of Rights is the heartbeat of our Constitution. It embodies the Liberal view of respect for the dignity of every individual"* and that the Liberal Party has "solved the financial problems of the past. The result is an economy that is the strongest and healthiest it's been in decades." Only his good little followers from within his Liberal girls' and boys' club could take this seriously.

Our Prime Minister should do his job to the best of his ability, based on what's best for the honest, hardworking people of this country. If he lacks that ability, then he should resign, not beg Canadians to give him another chance. We all have to answer to someone. Accountability is something this government knows absolutely nothing about.

The politicians have turned the simplest tasks into the most complicated structures as a way of protecting themselves. Why do we tolerate this?

Maybe what some of these politicians need is a little dose of reality? Maybe they should spend a month walking in the shoes of a police officer and experience the danger and devastation first-hand: face a knife-wielding maniac up close and personal; comfort a woman who's been beaten to a pulp while her child cowers in a closet, mute from fear; sit in a courtroom beside the family of a son or daughter who's been brutally murdered or raped, and view the family's shock and dismay when a judge hands down a meagre sentence; attend parole board hearings, where victims and their families plead for a perpetrator's continued sentence. This is reality, and I doubt they have what it takes to venture into the real world. But perhaps this is the only way they'll get serious about change.

Change is not only warranted, but also essential to the health of this great nation. The sponsorship scandal, the gun registry fiasco, the bonus system, all point to one thing: the Liberal Government has failed us. An election is due.

Canada's Prime Minister isn't the only politician who deserves flagellation. Bruce Miller, Liberal Opposition Caucus Member, Edmonton-Glenora, stated that "now is not the time to talk about issues that we must face in the future, like the under-funding of our police service in Alberta and dealing with gangs." When is the time to discuss this and related issues? When the next tragedy occurs, or perhaps the one after that? And then there's Bruce Hogle, Chairman of the Alberta Press Council, who has his priorities completely backwards. He wants the province of Alberta and Government of Canada, along with residents and RCMP detachments of Whitecourt and Mayerthorpe, to "immediately promise to provide the funding necessary to establish permanent community-oriented facilities in each community, in lasting honour of these four brave and wonderful RCMP personnel."

The RCMP and other law enforcement agencies don't have enough funding from the government to properly provide manpower and equipment, and Mr. Hogle wants millions spent on some buildings? To really honour these men, provide the necessary resources that should have saved their lives in the first place. I'm sure if you could call the boys in heaven and ask them what they think, they'd answer that their brothers join them later rather than sooner.

Alberta Liberal Leader Kevin Taft said the tragedy in Mayerthorpe is "a tragic puzzle" and that he hopes to "get a clear picture of how this could happen." It's a sad day in Canada when another Liberal politician can't see the forest for the trees.

Nick Taylor, former senator and one-time Alberta Liberal Leader, stuck his foot all the way down his throat at the Liberal Convention in Ottawa, when he suggested that Constables Schiemann, Myrol, Gordon and Johnston might be alive today if marijuana had been legalized. Only a Liberal could say something this asinine. Again, we are reminded of the lengths that some politicians will go to in order to further their political agenda. Such comments are reprehensible and offensive. This tragedy was not the consequence of a grow-op; it only added fuel to the fire. It was the consequence of a failing judicial system that is supposed to protect us from the violent offenders that are roaming our streets. The answer is not to decriminalize marijuana; we must tighten up law enforcement, increase the harshness of sentences and give the police the resources required to make it happen.

Alberta Solicitor General Harvey Cenaiko was disgusted that such a tragedy could occur over a marijuana grow-op. He said, "It goes to the seriousness of the fact that organized crime, illegal cultivation of marijuana or illegal production of crystal meth is all around us in the province." He also claimed to be "more committed than ever towards the dismantling of organized crime in every region of this province" and that "in the immediate future

[he] will be presenting a strategy to [his] government colleagues that will address this issue." Actions speak louder than words: the "immediate future" happened to be months ago. This is the same Harvey Cenaiko who, instead of dismantling organized crime in this province, is planning on dismantling and replacing the RCMP in this province by the year 2012. That's a really good strategy.

I would expect that recreational pot smokers will have something to say about this. It's time to face the facts: your pot smoking benefits organized crime and street gangs. It's likely the dealer is selling a variety of drugs such as crystal methamphetamine (a deadly, cheap and easy to make drug), ecstasy and crack, as well as buying illegal guns, which all contribute to the crime rate and disintegration of a society. Remember, they're also selling this crap to our children. But if you still choose to smoke, at least look in the mirror and take responsibility for your actions.

Deputy Prime Minister and Minister of Public Safety and Emergency Preparedness Anne McLellan has stated in the House of Commons that she'll consider tougher penalties for marijuana grow operations and that she and Justice Minister Irwin Cotler will review their proposed marijuana decriminalization bill to see if it goes far enough in dealing with growers. She also claimed that "there is no more important obligation for government than to provide its citizens with both individual and collective safety and security." She pledged to do more to give the RCMP the tools to do more, better and safer. She also conceded that police need more help and mentioned a "resource issue." She questioned, "Do we have the right laws in place?" "Have we given the RCMP and other forces the right tools they need to deal with what is an amazing growth, quite truthfully, in these operations?" In response to the Mayerthorpe tragedy, she said, "We are open to significant and wide-ranging amendments" and "we are putting the onus on the courts...to take this crime seriously. This is not a victimless crime and, therefore, I think the judiciary needs to start to reflect the harsh reality of illegal grow-ops."

You think? But this is the same government that pursued and then made drastic sentencing reform changes in 1996; the same government that created "conditional sentencing." Do the politicians really think that they can screw up like this and expect us to forget? Ms. McLellan speaks to the public with such emotion and conviction, but it was her government that asked for, and received, the lenient penalties. She got what "we" paid for.

How convenient for Ms. McLellan to blame the justice system and slap their fingers under the public glare of Canadian citizens. This time she needs to put our taxpayer money where her Liberal mouth is and do the right thing for a change. She needs to put Canadian citizens first and do what's best for them, not what's best for her own political agenda. Her Liberal wisdom to decriminalize marijuana and legalize prostitution will flush Canada down the toilet.

Ms. McLellan vowed that these four remarkable officers did not die in vain. She now has the chance to ensure that they did not. She now has the opportunity to inject real change into the judicial system. She asked some difficult questions and Canadians expect not only answers, but also results.

Stephen Harper, on the other hand, Leader of the Conservative Party, commented that the government "can't just run out on the basis of a single tragedy and make up a bunch of laws." This is not a single tragedy. James Roszko had very serious run-ins with the law over the past thirty-one years. His actions on March 3, 2005, were the culmination of over three decades of terror and fear felt by almost everyone who knew him or came into contact with him. There are hundreds of James Roszkos committing crimes, and, for the most part, getting away with them. Bob Mills, Red Deer Conservative MP, echoed my own sentiments when he said, "I think it was pretty obvious that this was a pretty dangerous person [James Roszko], so the justice system, I think, failed." Mr. Harper has blinders on. No one is asking him to "make up a bunch of laws." How about re-scripting existing ones so that these violent offenders actually spend some serious time in jail and are no longer a threat to society? Is that so much to ask?

Albert Premier Ralph Klein expressed his sadness about the slain officers. He called it "a crime of horrific proportions" and "that such unspeakable tragedy should befall them weighs heavily on the hearts of Albertans." Weeks after, he publicly announced on April 1, 2005, that Alberta was effectively debt-free. By the middle of April, the Alberta Government announced changes that would see provincial policing receive the biggest increase it has seen in years. Alberta will be getting one hundred new RCMP officers and an additional thirty police officers will be pulled out of administration and put onto the streets. The province will also provide funding for approximately sixty experienced officers to assist in fighting serious crime, which includes the methamphetamine problem and the increasing grow operations.

This may not be the answer to all of our prayers, but it's a positive step in the right direction.

All Canadians, and all Canadian politicians, owe these four men a bettered policing system. BC Premier Gordon Campbell said it best: "Together, as citizens and as a society, we must continue to seek an end to the threat and injustice drug-related crimes bring to our neighbour-hoods and communities across the country. That is precisely the goal these four officers were pursuing when they fell, and as Canadians we owe it to their memory to continue their work."

Thank you, Mr. Campbell.

Chapter 4 – The Justice System

"Law and justice are not always the same.

When they aren't, destroying the law may be

the first step toward changing it."

Gloria Steinem

"This is a court of law, young man,

not a court of justice."

Oliver Wendell Holmes, Jr.

Understanding the law and the ideas and principles behind it is every Canadian's business. The basis of much of our law is common sense, and ever since people began to live together in society, laws have been necessary to hold that society together. Laws are meant to ensure a safe and peaceful society in which people's rights are respected.

The Canadian legal system was implemented to respect individual rights, while at the same time ensuring that our society operates in an orderly manner. Our legal system, based on a tradition of law and justice, is meant to give Canadian society a valuable framework. The rule of law, freedom under the law, democratic principles and respect for others form the foundations of this important heritage.

Throughout the years, modern society has become increasingly complicated, and because of this, more laws are being enacted today than ever before. As people change the way they live and work, some laws become obsolete or new situations may arise that are not dealt with by any existing law. More than just changing laws, we may need to change the system of law and justice itself.

The people of Canada elect the lawmakers. We need to decide what we want from the law, and then ensure that it reflects those wishes. Everyone has the right to point out existing flaws in the law and to work towards appropriate changes. It seems to be, more so than ever before, that the time for change is now. The safety of our own selves, our children, families and friends is something we all cherish dearly. Canada is a great country, but we are proud people in a dangerous era.

Canada became a country by an act of the Parliament of Great Britain. Consequently, the closest thing to a constitutional document would be the *British North America Act of 1867 (the BNA Act)*. There is no single constitution in Canadian law, but the *Constitution Act* is a part of the

Canada Act of 1982. This constitution sets out the basic principles of democratic government in Canada when it defines the powers of three branches of government: the executive, the legislative and the judicial.

The *Canadian Bill of Rights*, passed in 1960, was the first federal law that specifically set the fundamental human rights for Canadians. *The Canadian Human Rights Act* (CHRA), first enacted in 1977, also protects human rights. Nevertheless, the protection provided by all of this legislation is limited, and it was not until the advent of the *Canadian Charter of Rights and Freedoms* that human rights were protected in the Constitution.

The *Canadian Charter of Rights and Freedoms* became a fundamental part of the Constitution in 1982. The Charter takes precedence over other legislation because it is "entrenched" in the Constitution, the supreme law of Canada. However, the Charter also recognizes that even in a democracy rights and freedoms are not absolute. The Charter protects fundamental freedoms, democratic rights, the right to move from one province or territory to another in Canada, legal, equality and language rights, and Aboriginal rights.

The Charter does not embody all our rights as Canadians; it only guarantees basic minimum rights.

In a nutshell, the Charter has been abused beyond the point of no return. Because of the way it is written and the grey areas surrounding certain parts of it, defence lawyers have, over the years, turned it into a pile of horse manure. They have taken every element and twisted it, warped it, mangled it, abused it and beat it into the ground. The evidence in most criminal cases no longer has the same meaning that it used to – evidence really means nothing if a loophole within the Charter sets a guilty person free. There is no such thing anymore as "let the evidence speak for itself."

Let's get down to the nuts and bolts of our wonderful justice system and see why and where the system has failed us miserably. In order to do that we need to look at how things actually work. The lawmakers – our government – have failed on a grand scale.

There are five major sectors of the Canadian justice system: policing, courts, legal aid, criminal prosecutions and adult corrections. Government spending with respect to these sectors is a very important issue.

A report from *Statistics Canada* for the year 2000/01 stated that in terms of the government sector, the year 2000 saw the largest budgetary surpluses in ten years and indicated that this favourable financial position helped encourage increases to government spending. That year, 30 percent of government spending went to social services, 16 percent to health care, 14 percent to education and 13 percent to debt charges.

Compared to ten years previous, however, spending on protection of persons and property went down (-11 percent). In total that year, government spending on the five major sectors amounted to $11 billion, or $362.00 per Canadian. The breakdown of the five sectors was as follows:

- Policing – $6.8 billion, an increase of 4 percent over the previous year and equals $221.00 per Canadian. However, it should be noted that this $6.8 billion was 4 percent below the cost for the exact same expenditures ten years ago.
- Adult Corrections – $2.5 billion, an increase of 1 percent over the previous year and equals $80.00 per Canadian.
- Courts – $1.0 billion, an increase of 4 percent since 1998/99 (last reported) and equals $34.00 per Canadian.

- Legal Aid – $512 million, an increase of 2 percent over the previous year and equals $17.00 per Canadian.
- Criminal Prosecution – $335 million, an increase of 15 percent since 1998/99 (last reported) and equals $11.00 per Canadian.

What was really interesting was that of the $11 billion, policing activities represented 61 percent, but we know now that none of this money was used for hiring and recruiting more frontline officers or to provide these officers with better equipment and resources.

Public Attitude toward the Justice System

Public attitude toward the criminal justice system is an issue that needs to be seriously addressed. People aren't complaining because they have nothing better to do; their expectations are not being met by the justice system. Society has the ability to influence the development of social policy, and it's time the government listened to our complaints.

Statistics Canada published a report in 1999, which adequately highlights Canadians' plummeting attitudes towards the criminal justice system and its courts, prison and parole systems. Even though this report reflects opinion from six years ago, it seems impossible that the statistics would have improved for the better. The highest level of public satisfaction with the courts was reported to be in 1988 – almost two decades ago.

Through academic research and polling results, it has been found that Canadians are confident in the police but are dissatisfied with other sectors of the justice system. For example, *Statistics Canada* stated that a recent *Environics* poll found Canadians have more confidence in the RCMP and local police than in the courts, lawyers, judges and parole boards. Less than one quarter of the population felt the criminal courts were doing a good job of determining whether or not the accused is guilty (21 percent), helping the victim (15 percent) and providing justice quickly (13 percent). Between 11 and 17 percent of Canadians did not have an opinion concerning the performance of the criminal courts.

In similar attitudes toward the courts, Canadians do not rate the prison and parole systems as positively as they do police. Only 26 percent of the population felt that the prison system was doing a good job of supervising and controlling prisoners, 14 percent felt that it was doing a good job at helping prisoners become law-abiding citizens and almost 30 percent of Canadians felt the prison system was doing a poor job at helping prisoners become law-abiding citizens.

As for the parole system, only 15 percent of the population believed it was doing a good job at releasing offenders who are not likely to re-offend, 13 percent believed it was doing a good job at supervising offenders on parole and 30 percent believed it was doing a poor job. Twenty percent of people were uncertain how to assess the performance of the parole system.

These statistics send a clear message to the government: Canadian citizens are not happy with the current system.

In contrast to these statistics, young Canadians ages fifteen to twenty-four were more satisfied with the criminal courts and felt that the prison and parole systems were doing a good job. It's very likely that this response is in direct relation to the fact that our courts tend to not punish our youth, or if they do, it's in a very minimal fashion.

Sentencing is just one of the many components of the criminal justice system that consistently attracts public criticism and concern. Members of the public are not satisfied with the criminal courts. These findings have emerged from Canadian public opinion polls for decades and are also reflected in surveys conducted not only in Canada, but in other countries as well.

Quebec residents were the strongest supporters of non-prison-based sanctions for all first-time adult offenders, with the exception of assault. On the other hand, the majority of Canadians believe that offenders who have criminal records should receive prison-based sanctions. With respect to young offenders and sentencing, 44 percent of Canadians support a prison sentence for repeat offences regardless of whether the offence was a break and enter or a minor assault.

Trends in Drug Offences and the Role of Alcohol and Drugs in Crime

Crystal methamphetamine is a highly addictive drug whose use has become terrifyingly common in recent years. This killer drug can be snorted or injected, or in its crystal form, smoked in a pipe, and brings on a feeling of exhilaration and sharp focus. Smoking meth results in an instantaneous dose of almost pure drug to the brain. The user experiences a huge "rush" followed by a feeling of great happiness that can last two to sixteen hours; the effects of meth can last six to eight hours.

After the initial "rush," there is typically a state of high agitation that, in some individuals, can lead to violent behavior. At low doses, meth boosts alertness and blocks hunger and fatigue. At higher doses, meth causes exhilaration. At very high doses, meth can cause agitation, paranoia and bizarre behaviour. Anxiety, emotional swings and paranoia are the most common psychological effects due to long-term use of meth. Symptoms increase with long-term use, and can involve paranoid delusions and hallucinations. Violence and self-destructive behaviour are common. The side effects of meth include paranoia, short-term memory loss, wild rages and mood swings as well as damage to the immune system – meth is extremely psychologically addictive.

Withdrawal, length and severity of depression is related to how much and how often meth is used. Withdrawal symptoms include cravings, exhaustion, depression, mental confusion, restlessness, insomnia and deep or disturbed sleep, all of which may last up to forty-eight hours.

An overdose can happen at relatively low levels. Metabolic rates vary from person to person, and the strength of the meth varies from batch to batch, so there is no way of stating a "safe" level of use. Methamphetamine addiction kills by causing heart failure, brain damage and stroke. For more information log on to http://searchnow180.com/sites/crystal_meth/crystal_meth_and_canada.html.

On August 12, 2005, the federal government announced new tougher penalties, including life in prison, for those involved in the production of crystal methamphetamine. Great news, except now we need someone in the justice system to enforce the penalties.

In the case of marijuana, many politicians want to change the legislation regarding offenders who are found in possession of small amounts of this drug. The government and justice system want to clear these charges from our existing court system because of the huge backlog that is preventing them from dealing with more serious criminal charges in an acceptable time frame. Some people agree and some people disagree. The bottom line is that marijuana is purchased from someone who is linked to organized crime. The violence and crime stems from that first initial purchase no matter how small: If 5000 people make a purchase of $50, it adds up to $250,000 of cold hard cash. It's usually gang members and/or organized crime groups reaping the rewards.

The rate of police-reported drug offences increased by 42 percent between 1992 and 2002, and much of the increase can be attributed to the rise in offences for the possession of marijuana. At the same time, this 42 percent increase also means the organized crime operators and/or gangs are making a hell of a lot more money – in turn, this means more crime and violence on the streets and more work for law enforcement agencies.

Police-reported statistics show that marijuana offences have also risen 81 percent between 1992 and 2002 – that's almost double over the past decade. Three in four drug-related offences were directly related to marijuana.

For those who may be unaware, marijuana purchased twenty years ago is not the same drug sold on the streets today. Today it is laced with various types of other drugs in order to give the user a much better high and to ensure that the user comes back for more. Unfortunately, the children and youth of this country, who think they're just smoking a little weed, are the ones who pay the heaviest price.

Drug-related violations in 2002 were the highest for individuals between the ages of eighteen and twenty-four (860 per 100,000 of population), followed by ages twelve to seventeen (645 per 100,000 population). Cocaine violations, including trafficking, were reported to be most common among the eighteen to twenty-four year olds. Pretty scary, isn't it?

Estimates from the 1999 *General Social Survey* suggest that in half of all physical (51 percent) and sexual (48 percent) assaults, the victim believes the incident was related to the perpetrator's use of drugs or alcohol.

In 2002, police reported about 81,000 incidents of impaired driving for people aged sixteen and over. Young drivers aged nineteen to twenty-four continue to have the highest rate for impaired driving and was a factor in almost half (47 percent) of all incidents causing death in 2002. Approximately 53,000 cases were heard in court during 2001/02, making it the largest offence category for that year (12 percent).

Between 1992 and 2002, 684 (11 percent) homicide incidents in Canada were reported to be drug-related. Of these, 176 (26 percent) were gang-related. Cocaine was the drug most commonly involved in homicide situations (60 percent) followed by marijuana (20 percent). Not such harmless stuff after all.

RCMP statistics for 2003 show that the estimated annual production of marijuana in Canada was over 800 tonnes, and the number of plants seized in Canada annually has exceeded 1,000,000 for the past four years. British Columbia, Ontario and Quebec, in particular, accounted for 88 percent of reported incidents in 2000. The estimated value of the marijuana industry in British Columbia is between $2 and $10 billion, making it one of BC's top three industries. On average, law enforcement agencies raid approximately two thousand BC grow operations per year – a rate of more than five per day.

The community usually suffers the economic losses with respect to residential marijuana grow operations (hydro and insurance costs are shared by rate-payers). The result is more crime in the area – violent and otherwise. The safety and health hazards are numerous (toxic mould for example), and then there's the contribution to decreased property and real estate values. It's also estimated that 65-98 percent of marijuana production is related to organized crime in Canada (Consulting and Audit Canada, 2002). Suburban Canada isn't nearly as safe as we think it is.

Drug and alcohol use have a complex association with crime. For example, while many adolescents begin their drug experience before committing illegal activities, a smaller portion begin using drugs only after becoming involved in non-drug criminal activity. In either case, the criminal activity is often used to fund their substance abuse (Brunelle, Brochu and Cousineau, 2000). Whether they're arrested for possession of drugs or not, violent crimes are, and will continue to be, committed to support their addiction – that is a statistical fact and it will not change any time soon if we don't do something about it.

In 2001/02, when a prison sentence was imposed in adult court for trafficking, only 42 percent of offenders were sent to prison, 30 percent were handed a probation sentence and 20 percent were fined. For drug possession, the statistics show that 12 percent were imprisoned, 28 percent received probation and 57 percent were fined. In total, 24 percent of convicted offenders went to jail, 29 percent went on probation and 42 percent were fined. Forget about what's wrong with this picture, what's right with it?

Our Failing Justice System – Significant Challenges

Notorious sex-killer Paul Bernardo's appeal on his first-degree murder conviction cost Ontario taxpayers over $150,000. What an outrage. No wonder the government spent five years trying to hide this fact from the public.

Something somewhere in the system has failed and continues on its course of destruction, and that makes it political. The government must punish criminals and crime in order to deter it. If the criminals don't behave themselves while in jail and get with the program, then they should stay there. The criminals need to prove that they deserve a second chance, not the other way around.

Why is it that a criminal's past criminal activity and/or record cannot be used in court? It stands to reason that the best indicator of future conduct is past behaviour. James Roszko's rap sheet should have sounded alarm bells a long time ago. This is just one example of how our justice system lacks the teeth to put the criminals behind bars.

We need a different system for the violent criminal element – one that works. We should start with a system that breaks down into two sectors: violent crimes and non-violent crimes. This seems to be the core issue and the big concern. Violent crimes should, without a shred of doubt, be the focal point. As it stands, there doesn't seem to be enough room to house the violent criminals because the non-violent criminals are taking up space. If there isn't enough money to build more prisons, then non-violent criminals need a different type of punishment.

It seems pretty simple: separate the two entities and deal with them differently because they're on opposite sides of the spectrum. If someone is stopped for speeding and has unpaid fines, the police should impound the vehicle until the fines are paid. Garnishee wages if need be – the government does it if you don't pay your taxes. If someone is arrested for stealing, then he or she should pay restitution, get fingerprinted and have a criminal record. Rather than spend time in jail, he or she could be sentenced to a work program, picking garbage in the ditch. Repeat offenders could be sent to prison after sentencing and put to work on behalf of society – perhaps plant and harvest 5000 rows of potatoes for the food bank to assist those less fortunate. The more times the system has to deal with an individual, the tougher the sentence gets. At some point they will get the picture.

The violent criminals need to have a different system in place. The punishment has to fit the crime; they have one shot at rehabilitation, not three or four. If they physically hurt someone then they go to prison. No slap on the wrist, no probation, no conditional sentencing, no day passes, no conjugal visits with a significant other. While these criminals are in prison they must be required to get with the program: counseling, anger management and perhaps volunteering for Victim Services. Allow them the opportunity to make things right. If they refuse to cooperate, then that's the end of the line. They stay in prison for the remainder of their sentence. The system is supposed to protect us, not continually put us in harm's way.

If the violent criminals cooperate and complete the required programs and sentence, then they should be cautiously released with the proper conditions and considered to have paid their debt to society. If they end up back in prison for another violent crime, then they do their time. No second chances. Some offenders cannot be, and do not want to be, rehabilitated. These are the people that have proved to society that they should not be released, and we should be protected from them. This is ultimately where the danger lies, and history has proved it time and time again.

Activists and human rights people will be up in arms, but they should also button their lips sometimes. If they could spend time with a victim of violent crime, they might gain a different perspective. When a convicted criminal has taken away another person's rights, that criminal, in turn, should also have certain rights taken away. How can it possibly be fair, right and just to allow these criminals to, for example, engage in conjugal three-day visits with their significant other in a two-bedroom unit provided at the expense of taxpaying citizens? The prisoners lose nothing while the victims' have been stripped of everything they hold sacred: their sense of safety, well-being and emotional security.

The punishment for those that commit horrendous acts of violence versus those that are not a threat to society has to be defined. Where's the logic when someone who steals money from shareholders or files a false insurance claim is sentenced to decades in prison, and someone who rapes, sells drugs, robs a bank or commits murder gets only a couple of years combined with conditional sentences, probation and day passes? Don't get me wrong – breaking the law is breaking the law, but the difference is like comparing fire and water.

Because of the way our justice system currently stands and the lack of funding and resources for our law enforcement officers in Canada, the criminal element has nothing to fear – it has all been stripped away. Thirty years ago, when things were different, there was always a certain amount of fear and it was required in order to keep the peace. That healthy fear kept many of us out of trouble and out of jail. Today's troubled youth have no respect, and most certainly no fear of consequences. They will not have a criminal record and will not receive jail time. Instead, they are granted extra-judicial sanctions (punishment outside of the court process) and restorative justice (an approach that focuses on repairing the harm caused by crime while holding the offender responsible for his or her actions). Fear of consequences needs to return in order to gain some control over the large number of juvenile offenders.

Funds to Increase the Security and Protection of Canadians

In October 2001, in the wake of the September 11 attack on the United States, the federal government announced an immediate $64 million in funding to the RCMP as follows:

- $10.3 million – to enhance security at airports, major centers, ports and border crossings.
- $35.0 million – to enhance the ability of the RCMP to gather, analyze, assess and share intelligence and investigative information through new technologies, better technical and operational support and improved infrastructure systems.
- $9.0 million – annually to staffing priorities such as the Integrated National Security Enforcement Teams and Integrated Border Enforcement Teams.
- $5.0 million – to support deployment of RCMP to protect designated persons and sites in Canada.
- $4.9 million – to the Solicitor General of Canada to develop and implement the Canada Public Safety Information Network (CPSIN), a national information network linking various criminal justice, enforcement and national security agencies.

No spending went into protecting Canadian citizens from the crime on the streets. It looks great to the rest of the world, but I guess our frontline officers don't measure up in the big scheme of things. At this moment, I'm a lot more afraid of the crime on the streets than I am of a terrorist attack on Canada. The terrorists already live here in Canada; maybe if there were more police on the streets they might be easier to find.

In the budget announced on December 10, 2001, the feds presented a five-year $7.7 billion funding strategy for initiatives intended to improve the safety and protection of Canadians. For instance:

- $1.6 billion – spread over five years and allocated to strengthening intelligence and policing. This intelligence and policing effort will provide monies to improve information-sharing capabilities among law enforcement, intelligence and national security agen-

cies to increase the number of police intelligence officers and to see that these officers are better equipped.

- $2.2 billion – dedicated to measures to improve the
  safety of air travel and implement new air security
  measures.
- $1.2 billion – to enhance the security and efficiency of
  the Canada-U.S. border and the creation of more
  Integrated Border Enforcement Teams.

In total, about $8.3 million, according to this report, was
allocated almost specifically to "federal and international
operations." In plain English, almost every dime went
straight into the province of Ontario, where RCMP head-
quarters is located. It's so disappointing, again, to see that
the rest of Canada is so meaningless to the federal government.

Justice Revenues for Policing

In 1989, legislation was passed allowing the RCMP to
confiscate wealth (e.g., money, vehicles, houses, jewellery)
acquired through illicit activities. Seized assets are held
pending the outcome of judicial procedures. If the courts
determine that assets are to be forfeited, the proceeds from
these forfeitures go to the government, which can in turn,
use these revenues to fund social and other programs.

Forfeiture proceeds totaled $10.7 million and the RCMP
Integrated Proceeds of Crime (IPOC) units impounded
assets valued at approximately $23.6 million. (It should be
noted that forfeitures are dependent on the decisions of
the court. Confiscated assets may not result in forfeiture if
charges are dismissed before the case goes to trial or if
there is no conviction. As well, it may take two or three
years for a case to come to trial, thereby delaying the time
between asset seizure and forfeiture.)

The government is not obligated to use this money for social and other programs, hence the word "can" not "is." I believe the federal government has misled us again. All of this money should be going directly back into law enforcement agencies across Canada. At this moment, we don't know where it's going.

Justice System Funding and Victims of Crime

Alberta Justice Minister Ron Stevens announced on April 16, 2005, that new funding of more than $30 million that will be dispersed throughout Alberta Justice over the next three years will be used for initiatives such as counseling and mediation so that Albertans will have better access to justice services.

The breakdown for the funding is as follows:

- Family Justice Services – $7.9 million
- Specialized Family Violence Prosecutors – $6.8 million
- Video-conferencing in courtrooms – $2.0 million
- Compensation to interpreters and witnesses – $1.6 million
- Civil mediation – $2.4 million
- Medical Examiner's Office – $2.2 million
- Electronic Distribution of Court Briefs – $1.1 million
- Information Document Management – $0.8 million
- Information Technology Sustainability – $5.6 million

It's really nice to see all this money going into the justice system, but if it wasn't failing miserably, we wouldn't need to pump this kind of money into these specific areas. This $30 million could have provided Alberta with an additional one hundred police officers and paid their salaries for the next seven-and-a-half years.

Funding For Victims of Crime in Canada

Statistics Canada reported that in March 2000, the federal government committed $25 million over a five-year period to victim-related initiatives in order to address the needs of "victims of crime." As part of this commitment, $15 million is dedicated to consultation, research and public education on victims' rights. The other $10 million ($2 million per year for five years) is dedicated to the Victim's Fund that was established in August 2000, with the following objectives:

- To promote public awareness of victimization and its effects;
- To improve access to and participation in the justice system;
- To identify and develop programs to fill in the gaps;
- To enhance the role of community and non-governmental organizations as service providers, to build networks to improve service delivery, and to increase the involvement of community and non-governmental organizations in policy and legislation development;
- To provide financial support to family members of homicide victims as well as limited emergency funding to victims when other financial assistance is unavailable;
- To promote the implementation of legal reforms that address victims' needs;
- To promote the implementation of the Canadian Statement of Basic Principles of Justice for Victims of Crime.

Fifteen million dollars dedicated to consultation, research and public education on victims' rights is not an intelligent decision. Why is this money not being used where it's needed, to provide services for the victims?

My research indicates a horrible lack of services to assist these victimized people. As far as I can tell, this is another futile attempt from the federal government to make themselves look good in the eyes of Canadians and abroad. All of this money should be directly implemented into counseling, support groups and financial assistance for the victims or immediate family members of, who may need to travel in order to be with a victim or for other financial needs.

Ten million dollars is a tiny drop in the bucket over a five-year period between thirteen provinces and territories. According to my calculations, this amounts to not even $70,000 per year per province/territory. What a slap in the face to victims and victim service organizations across this country.

April 2002 Report of the Auditor General (Sheila Fraser)

Chapter four of this report indicated that major information gaps about the criminal justice system were standing in the way of a comprehensive assessment of the system's overall effectiveness. The report pointed to the need for better co-ordination and sharing of information on crime and offenders by the agencies and institutions that make up the criminal justice system and the steps being taken to address this issue. The Auditor General called for an assessment of the overall effectiveness of government efforts to reshape the criminal justice system.

Some important main points in the report that Canadians need to be aware of:

4.6 – According to federal government agencies, the system's capacity to maintain a high standard of public safety is under severe strain.

4.18 – Youths. About 33 percent more youths were charged with violent crime in 2000 than ten years ago, an increase of 7 percent after four years of decline. Youth courts heard about 102,000 cases in 1999-2000, involving 60,000 youths.

4.35 – Plea Bargaining. That plea bargaining occurs is widely acknowledged. The Federal Prosecution Service Desk Book of the Department of Justice indicates that several things can be negotiated: charges, procedure, sentences and the facts of an offence for the purpose of a guilty plea.

4.36 – Plea bargaining can have severe consequences:

- It can allow prosecutors and the courts to handle more cases with the same or fewer staff, reserving court time for more serious cases.
- It can give the prosecution and defence counsel significant control over the trial process and the outcome.
- It can save the victim from having to testify.
- A less serious charge can go on the offender's record, an important consideration should charges be laid for other incidents in the future.
- It can reduce the number of inmates in jail and thus the costs of building prisons and incarcerating offenders.

4.37 – The practice of plea bargaining has been criticized. It has the potential to undermine the integrity of the criminal justice system, in part because disclosure of the basis for agreements and accountability for the decisions has been inadequate. There are no reliable data on how often plea bargaining occurs and with what outcome.

4.41 – Victims. In 1983, a federal-provincial task force conducted the first study of justice for the victims of crime. It concluded that often the victim is "twice victimized: once by the offence and once more by the process."

4.46 – Impact. A 1998 study by the Solicitor General of Canada estimated the impacts of organized crime in Canada as the following:

- The value of the Canadian illicit drug market is between $7 billion and $10 billion each year. The RCMP's estimates to Parliament for 2000/01 indicated that the annual street value of illicit drugs could be as high as $18 billion.
- Economic crime, such as securities fraud and tele-marketing scams, costs Canadians at least $5 billion a year.
- Between $5 and $17 billion is laundered in Canada each year.
- Up to 16,000 people may be smuggled into Canada every year.
- The production and sale of counterfeit products such as clothing, software and pharmaceuticals could cost Canadians over $1 billion each year.
- Illegal smuggling of tobacco, alcohol and jewellery could result in the loss of up to $1.5 billion in government tax revenues.

4.49 – Preliminary data indicate that there are sixty-four large-scale organized crime groups in Canada. Most have national and international links that are used to exchange goods, services, expertise, skills, personnel and facilities. Most use legitimate businesses to launder money. About half are involved in the corruption of politics, the media, public administration, judicial authorities or the economy.

4.73 – To deal with drug abuse, Correctional Service Canada has focused on reducing the supply of drugs and alcohol in institutions and reducing the demand through program and health interventions. It re-instituted random urinalysis at all institutions in November 1992, and in 1994 it adopted a formal drug strategy.

4.98 – In July 2001, the Solicitor General of Canada reported the results of consultations with crime victims and providers of services to victims. The consultations indicated that victims' perceptions have not changed much since 1983. Victims still feel that offenders have more rights than victims; they want a larger voice in the process; they want respect; and they continue to live in fear.

4.132 – While at least $10 billion is spent each year on the criminal justice system, the government allocates only about $5 million to *Statistics Canada's Centre for Justice Statistics* (CCJS) for the collection of core national data on the system.

4.134 – The criminal justice data that are available have major gaps, such as the following:

- There is not enough information on Aboriginal people in the criminal justice system.
- Not enough information is available on restorative justice programs, diversion programs and victims' programs.
- Not enough information is available on the extent to which Canadians perceive that they have been victims of criminal behaviour.
- Information on organized crime is scarce, including data on the proportion of crime that is committed by criminal organizations.
- The RCMP provides aggregate but not detailed statistics on crime data; full and detailed coverage is expected in 2007.

- There are no data available on crimes investigated by private security personnel without the involvement of public police agencies.
- Military police and some First Nations police do not yet report crime statistics.
- New Brunswick, Manitoba and British Columbia do not report data on adult court activities; nor do about 140 municipal courts in Quebec.

In addition, the Department of Justice indicated that the absence of superior court data from most jurisdictions represents a major gap in the picture of how the justice system is functioning.

4.135 – Data on individuals as they pass from one criminal justice agency to another are also insufficient.

4.143 – The business of organized crime is lucrative and a major threat to the well-being of Canadians.

4.144 – There is a clear need for criminal justice agencies to improve their sharing of information on crime, offenders and victims.

If the Auditor General of Canada reports indicate where the problems are, it becomes clear that the situation is serious. The federal government appears to have time and money for everything on their agenda, but not for what is really important to the citizens of our country. The justice system and its failings have been questioned for years.

The Inevitable Conclusion

I read the newspaper every day like most Canadians, but there are often articles that stand out like a rose bush in the onion patch. Letters to the editor are my favourite. I often cut them out and tape them to the fridge door as a reminder of the importance I found in the words of some brilliant person. This particular letter was published in the

Calgary Sunday Sun on August 14, 2005, and clearly expresses the negligence of Canada's judicial system.

Country is full of contradictions

WHAT A sham our 'justice' system has become in this once great country. You can throw your newborn baby in the garbage and get off scot-free, but go to jail if you throw a pie at a politician. You can leave your loaded handgun in your car to be stolen by criminals and get off scot-free, but can't leave your pet in your car on a hot day. You can enter the country illegally, commit serious offences and our government refuses to deport you. You can get needles and drugs from the government for free if you're a junkie, but not if you're a diabetic. No wonder so many cultures think we have a decadent society, because we are.

Lance Gould

It's time for Canadians to use the voice that we have been given as a rite of passage through our citizenship and as taxpayers. Stand up, be heard and make a difference. We, the people, have made this great country what it is today; the politicians are destroying it, bit by bit. It is time for the politicians to know and understand that we want our country put back together again in the framework it originated from. A foundation built on honesty, truth and the ability to help everyone around us when called upon to do so. A foundation built on our faith in God, our fellow man and knowing the difference between right and wrong and doing something about it.

Canada is a peaceful and giving country because of the people that have chosen to live in it and raise their families here. The violence and evil that exist in this country is not welcome, but it exists nevertheless. It crept in, rooted itself and has spread like a rampant virus that is slowly killing and destroying everything in its path. It feeds on our children, our families, our morals and our values; it is fueled by the lack of responsibility in our government and the justice system. There is only one way to deal with a parasite of epidemic proportions such as this: get rid of it, or at least contain and control it.

We must do whatever is necessary, whether that means changing our government, changing our justice system or changing the laws and policies that govern it. It doesn't matter what the violent crime is, who the perpetrator is or where it happened. That leaves us with one simple question: Will our government listen to us?

Chapter 5 – Prisons in Canada

"Significant problems cannot be solved at the

same level of thinking that created them."

Albert Einstein

"We don't give our criminals much punishment,

but we sure give 'em plenty of publicity."

Will Rogers

Prisons, as defined by the Wikipedia free encyclopedia, are a place where people are confined and deprived of a range of liberties (freedoms). Prisons conventionally are institutions authorized by governments and forming part of a country's criminal justice system. Justice is the quality of being just; the administration of the law. These are two very important things required to work in unison towards the protection of citizens in the majority of countries around the world. Unfortunately, when failure occurs, the consequences can be, and often are, tragic.

On June 17, 1988, eleven-year-old Christopher Stephenson was kidnapped from a Brampton shopping mall near Toronto, Ontario. His kidnapper was forty-five-year-old Joseph Fredericks, a convicted pedophile out on parole after a long history of convictions for violent sexual assaults. Fredericks took Christopher to his room, where he tortured and raped him over a twenty-four-hour period. Fredericks then took Christopher to a wooded area where he murdered him.

None of these assaults appeared on Frederick's criminal record; partly because many of the sexual assaults occurred while he was a psychiatric patient, and partly because of plea-bargaining in other cases. Since then, new legislation was pursued by Christopher's father (Jim Stephenson), and became effective in Ontario on April 23, 2001 – Christopher's Law was enacted whereby, the act requires anyone convicted of a sexual offence to register at the local police station providing their name, date of birth, offence record and current address.

On November 22, 2002, the Edmonton Police Service issued a news release in the interest of public safety. The crucial information in this release stated the following:

> Karl Richard TOFT has now completed more than two-thirds of his thirteen-year sentence for numerous

convictions of sexual assault, buggery, and indecent assault and is currently residing at a Community Correctional Centre in Edmonton. TOFT will be allowed unaccompanied/ unescorted absences into the community on occasion as part of his gradual release into the community.

Due to a number of factors, the most important including the high number of victims, estimated to be more than 200 young male victims aged twelve to seventeen years, and a life-long history of sexually offending against children, TOFT is still considered by Edmonton Police Service to be a risk of significant harm to the community.

On March 20, 2005, Karla Homolka, convicted of manslaughter and sentenced to twelve years in prison, grabbed the headlines again with her impending release. God help us all. Joe Wamback of the Canadian Crime Victim Foundation said, "Karla isn't the first dangerous offender who's been released – the list goes on and on – and just look at what happens, look at how many of them re-offend." Wamback said there are 90,000 people in Ontario who are listed as "under supervision," including people on probation, parole and conditional release. There are only 900 officers to monitor them. "You don't need to be a rocket scientist to add it up. Canada is virtually at the bottom of the list in the industrialized world in protecting its citizens from released criminals," he said.

In April 2005, information was publicly released that Jean Guy Tremblay, a brutal psychopath and serial woman abuser, would be released from jail, having completed his undeniably short sentence of five years, followed by ten years of community service. Tremblay had fifteen convictions for violent offences, ranging from assault to unlawful confinement, before his conviction for abusing women.

The parole board has applied four conditions to his release. A parole board member, Mike Haklo, said the board was worried about Tremblay's release. Detective Jim MacDougall, who arrested Tremblay in 1999, now a director with the Calgary Police Association, said, "He's a psychopath, and my understanding is psychopaths are untreatable."

Another incident occurred in April, 2005, when it came to light that a convicted sex offender was placed in a group home right across the street from an Edmonton elementary school. Complaints were registered from neighbours and school officials after a man residing at the group home was spotted exposing himself. Provincial officials apologized and said it would not happen again.

These atrocities are an injustice perpetrated by Canada's failing justice system.

Throughout our prison and correctional system there have been many failures that could have been preventable. The federal government has feebly attempted to address some of the failures, but a band-aid is not the solution. Canadians need to better understand the situation we're facing in order to make some informed decisions.

Canada's federal penitentiaries house offenders who are sentenced to two or more years in prison and have committed serious offences. Offenders that are sentenced to less than two years are the responsibility of provincial or territorial correctional services. All of them fall under Correctional Service of Canada (CSC).

Adult Correctional Services only deals with persons eighteen years of age or older. This government body has six primary responsibilities:

1. Custodial Remand

In layman's terms, "held without bail." This happens when a person has been charged with an offence and is jailed while waiting for the next step of the judicial process. This decision is made by a judge based on factors such as do they pose a risk to the community? Is there a possibility they might re-offend? Are they a flight risk?

The onus is supposed to be on those accused as to why they feel they should be released in the meantime. If cause to keep them in custody is not established, then they are released with or without bail until the next court appearance. Unfortunately, too often dangerous criminals are put back on the streets, endangering the lives and safety of ordinary citizens. This is an outrage and needs to be addressed.

2. Custodial Sentences

This is the term used when someone charged with an offence is found guilty. This does not mean the guilty party is going to jail. Once guilt has been determined, the actual disposition is at the discretion of the presiding judge. The Criminal Code specifies the maximum for most offences, and in some instances a minimum punishment is also specified. *Statistics Canada* stated that, in Canada, the maximum sentence is rarely imposed and that the use of incarceration is usually limited to very serious offences and to repeat offenders.

I'm a little confused now. We have maximum sentences because there is a serious need for them, so why aren't we using them?

3. Conditional Sentences

Introduced in 1996, conditional sentences allow offenders sentenced to a term of custody to serve their time in the community under supervision. Conditional sentences may be imposed at the discretion of the presiding judge, though under certain restrictions. First, there must be no minimum term of imprisonment associated with the conviction(s). Second, the term of imprisonment that would normally have been imposed must be less than two years. Finally, the court must be satisfied that the imposition of a conditional sentence would not endanger the safety of the public. The objective is to provide less serious offenders with effective, less costly, community-based alternatives while using scarce-needed funds for the incarceration and treatment of more serious offenders.

There are of course compulsory conditions attached to conditional sentences, including remaining within the jurisdiction of the court and reporting to a supervisor as specified. Other conditions may require the offender to abstain from the consumption of alcohol or to perform community work. Should the offender fail to abide by the conditions, he or she can be returned to a court at which time the judge can suspend the conditional sentence and impose a jail term.

The law is saying that a criminal "may" be punished, not that he "will" be punished. This is asinine, and typical of the Liberal government. The changing of one or two simple words will send a clear message, unlike the vastly large grey cloud that currently surrounds the legislation.

4. Conditional Release

The planned and gradual release of inmates back into the community through "conditional release" is also the responsibility of correctional services. The use of various mechanisms helps to ensure the protection of society through the supervision of offenders while they're in the community. Supervision is administered by federal and provincial/territorial correctional systems.

The mechanisms for conditional release in Canada are as follows:

- Temporary Absence – allows offenders to leave the institution for specific purposes. Offenders may be either "escorted" or "unescorted." Releases are usually granted for family visits, medical services, rehabilitation programs, socialization or humanitarian reasons.

"Escorted" and "unescorted" absences for federal offenders are handed out more often then you might think. In 2002/03, the National Parole Board grant rate for both types of absences was 82.8 percent and 74.2 percent, respectively. From 2000/01 to 2002/03, forty-six inmates granted an "escorted temporary absence" were unlawfully at large, and 246 inmates granted an "unescorted temporary absence" were unlawfully at large. Some of these inmates were serving time for murder, armed robbery and sexual assault.

I think it's fair to say that Canada's inmates are being allowed to take advantage of the judicial system. How can the Liberal Government disregard public safety in such a blatant manner? How does Anne McLellan, the person in charge of Adult Correctional Services in Canada, sleep at night?

There are serious implications attached to these statistics. Below are alarming examples taken from five Canadian provinces of inmates who escaped during a lawfully permitted temporary absence. Also included are inmates who were on work release programs and those who were given a second chance and allowed to live in residential facilities or centres for the remainder of their sentences. Whether these criminals were re-captured is moot. The fact that they escaped in the first place is of major concern.

Nova Scotia

March 2, 2004: Truro – A twenty-nine-year-old inmate serving a second federal sentence of four years for various non-violent property-related offences such as theft, theft of credit cards, failure to comply, attempt to commit robbery, attempt to commit armed robbery and possession of a weapon was discovered missing during an escorted temporary absence for family contact purposes.

August 23, 2004: Springhill – A forty-three-year-old inmate serving a twenty-six year sentence for armed robbery and possession of a weapon fled while on an escorted temporary absence.

Quebec

January 16, 2004: Laval – A thirty-nine-year-old inmate serving a sentence of three years, four months, twenty-five days for fraud, theft under $5000 and various minor offences escaped while on an escorted temporary absence while attending a meeting.

April 26, 2004: Montreal – A forty-year-old inmate serving a seven-year sentence for sexual assault causing bodily harm and possession of drugs was granted statutory release with a residency requirement and failed to return to the centre where he was residing.

May 22, 2004: Montreal – A twenty-seven-year-old inmate who was under a long-term supervision order (extended length of time CSC can supervise and support a sex offender in the community beyond the completion of his or her regular sentence) after being sentenced to three years for sexual assault left the centre where he was residing.

July 22, 2004: Laval – A sixty-five-year-old inmate serving a life-sentence for non-capital murder failed to return at the site designated on his unescorted temporary absence pass.

August 31, 2004: Laval – A forty-three-year-old inmate serving a sentence of three years, nine months, thirteen days for theft over $5000, fraud, possession of break-in instruments and various failures to comply with orders disappeared while on an unescorted temporary absence.

September 7, 2004: Ste-Anne-Des-Plaines – A thirty-three-year-old inmate serving a sentence of seven years, four months, twenty-nine days for a variety of offences, including several charges of theft, possession of property obtained by crime, fraud and dangerous driving disappeared while on a work release to perform community service.

September 13, 2004: Montreal – A forty-five-year-old inmate deemed a long-term offender and under a long-term supervision order of ten years, serving a sentence of three years, two months, twenty-eight days for sexual assault, uttering threats and failure to comply, was granted statutory release with a residency requirement when he failed to return to his residence.

October 8, 2004: St-Jerome – A fifty-two-year-old inmate serving an eight-year sentence for sexual offences was granted statutory release with a residence requirement and failed to return to the centre where he was residing.

November 11, 2004: Montreal – A thirty-three-year-old inmate serving a six year, six month sentence for attempted murder, assault and firearms use was granted statutory release with a residence requirement. On the same day the residency began, the inmate failed to return to the facility.

November 22, 2004: Montreal – A forty-six-year-old inmate serving an eighteen-year sentence in a federal penitentiary for sex offences involving adult females was granted statutory release with a residence requirement when he failed to return to the residence.

December 24, 2004: Montreal – A twenty-four-year-old inmate serving a sentence of two years for break and enter, and four years, three months for sexual assault, abduction of a minor, aggravated assault and threatened bodily harm, was granted statutory release with a residence requirement when he failed to return to the centre where he was residing.

February 18, 2005: Laval – A forty-two-year-old inmate serving a life sentence for second degree murder, robbery and various failures to comply with orders escaped from custody while on an escorted temporary absence for medical reasons.

April 11, 2005: Laval – A fifty-five-year-old inmate incarcerated for various offences including arson and manslaughter fled the location where he was performing community work.

May 19, 2005: Laval – A thirty-eight-year-old inmate serving a four-year sentence for robbery and possession of a weapon escaped while on an escorted temporary absence for medical reasons.

May 30, 2005: Ste-Anne-Des-Plaines – A forty-seven-year-old inmate serving a sentence of three years, six months, twenty days for a variety of offences including several counts of break and enter, possession of a break-in instrument and being unlawfully in a dwelling house escaped from an escorted temporary absence for medical reasons.

Ontario

March 2, 2004: Kingston – A forty-one-year-old inmate serving a sentence of four years, six months for robbery and fraud escaped custody while on an escorted temporary absence to attend a funeral.

British Columbia

May 6, 2004: Mission – An inmate serving a six-year sentence for possession of property obtained by crime, dangerous operation of a motor vehicle and break and enter escaped while on an escorted temporary absence to attend a meeting.

Alberta

January 11, 2004: Drumheller – A twenty-two-year-old inmate serving a five-year sentence for three counts of robbery escaped while on a seventy-two-hour family contact unescorted temporary absence.

March 23, 2004: Edmonton – A thirty-one-year-old inmate serving a three year, nine month sentence for robbery, attempted robbery and theft failed to return to the facility from a work release.

May 10, 2004: Edmonton – A thirty-one-year-old inmate serving a two year, one month, fourteen day sentence for break and enter and other property offences was released in the community on a pass. The inmate failed to return to the centre.

March 1, 2005: Edmonton – A forty-three-year-old inmate serving an aggregate sentence of twenty-one years, six months for robbery failed to return to the facility from work release.

- Day Parole – provides offenders with the opportunity to participate in ongoing community-based activities. Ordinarily, offenders reside at a correctional institution or community residence and are released into the community for a specified period of time during the day. Offenders are also granted day parole in order to prepare them for full parole and statutory release.

- Full Parole – is granted at the discretion of paroling authorities (parole board).

This allows offenders to serve part of their prison sentence in the community. In all instances, offenders are placed under supervision by a parole officer and are required to abide by conditions designed to reduce the risk of re-offending and to foster re-integration into the community.

- Statutory Release – allows most federally sentenced inmates who have not been granted parole to serve the final third of their sentence under supervision in the community and under conditions of release similar to those imposed on offenders released on full parole.

So, here we go again. If a criminal is denied parole, obviously the parole board had some very good reasons for doing so. How can the system then justify allowing federal inmates (the most serious offenders) who are denied parole to serve out the final third of their sentence under supervision in the community? It's like the system is making up for denying parole. It's sheer lunacy.

5. Probation

Probation is the responsibility of correctional services and is a sentence served in the community in which the offender "may" or "may not" be required to report to a probation officer. Terms of probation that do not require supervision do not generally come to the attention of correctional authorities. For the purpose of this information, the use of the term "probation" will refer to supervised probation only.

6. Parole Boards

Quebec, Ontario and British Columbia have jurisdiction for all offenders in their own provincial institutions. The National Parole Board has jurisdiction over all offenders serving out sentences (of two or more years) in penitentiaries and offenders in provincial/territorial correctional facilities where no parole board exists. Parole boards have the power and authority to grant, deny, terminate or revoke parole in their jurisdictions. The National Parole Board also has the power and authority to terminate or revoke offenders on "statutory release," detain certain offenders and grant "unescorted temporary absences" for some offenders in penitentiaries.

James Roszko's parole board hearings were contradictory and, quite frankly, bizarre. On February 6, 2001, the parole board denied Roszko's request because he presented "an undue risk to re-offend." They also advised that there was some concern about his ability to "function over the long term in a manner consistent with the protection of the community." Ten months later, in December, he was granted parole and released from prison. Five months later, in May, his parole was suspended for not cooperating with his parole officer, and seven days later he was arrested. Three months later, the parole board said that Roszko's risk "remains manageable in the community."

Historically speaking, how did Roszko's behaviour go from very bad to "manageable in the community"? The incomprehensible loss of Alberta's four RCMP officers was not only at the hands of James Roszko, but also at the hands of our justice system.

Criminals should be given one chance. If they blow it, then they should be classified as "unable to rehabilitate" and remain in jail for the balance of their sentence. Criminals need to prove, via the strictest of criteria, that they should be allowed a shot at parole. Right now our system does nothing of the kind. The parole board gives "get out of jail free cards" more often than a game of Monopoly.

Statistics for Adult Correctional Facilities in Canada

It's important to discuss some of the statistics directly related to the offenders that are housed in Canadian facilities. There is nothing currently available after the year 1996, but this report still provides Canadians with a good idea of who's there, why and for how long. It also gives us a really good idea of the risks to society that are associated with assessments done by CSC of whether these inmates are at a low, medium or high risk of re-offending when released. The information provided in this report is basically a "snapshot" (one-day survey) of inmates in Canada's adult correctional facilities.

On October 5, 1996, there were forty-eight adult federal correctional facilities operating in Canada. The total operational capacity (permanent beds) was 12,921 – an average of 269 inmates per facility. Of the forty-eight facilities, twenty were classified as medium security, ten as maximum security, twelve as minimum security and six as "multi-level" security.

On snapshot day, a total of 13,862 inmates were on-register across Canada. Based on this calculation, these facilities were over-capacity by 7 percent and over one-half of these (56 percent) were operating above the rated capacity. However, it is noted that both minimum- and multi-level facilities were operating under-capacity (92 percent and 90 percent respectively). It was the medium- and max-imum- (111 percent and 113 percent respectively) security facilities that were operating over-capacity. This report also stated that 72 percent of federal inmates were being accommodated in single cells; the other 28 percent were being double-bunked.

This is the best indicator currently available that tells Canadians that the need for medium- and maximum-security prisons has to be addressed. These are the most dangerous offenders in Canada! If we're going to keep them off the streets, we need somewhere to put them. Is the National Parole Board of Canada paroling dangerous offenders because of over-crowding? Why do the majority of federal inmates have the privilege of a single cell?

The most serious offence for 73 percent of inmates was for a crime against a person, primarily homicide/attempt-ed murder and robbery; followed by 15 percent for prop-erty offences, primarily break and enter; and 11 percent for "other" Criminal Code or Federal Statute offences, prima-rily drug-related offences.

The largest proportion of inmates were incarcerated for a total of five or more offences at 30 percent, followed by four offences at 11 percent, three offences at 14 percent, two offences at 19 percent and one offence at 26 percent.

On snapshot day, 50 percent were serving sentences of less than six years, 30 percent were serving sentences of between six and twenty years, and 2 percent were serving sentences of a fixed length of twenty or more years. An additional 18 percent of inmates were serving life sentences.

With all of the vicious and violent crimes in Canada, including homicides, attempted murder, robbery and drug trafficking, why on earth are 50 percent of inmates serving sentences of less than six years? I believe it's more than likely because the judges in this country don't know the meaning of "true" sentences (i.e., if you're sentenced to three years, you're imprisoned for three years), and they most definitely do not use the maximum sentences even though they're readily available.

The aggregate (sum total) sentence length for on-register inmates in 1996:

- Less than 2 years – 3 percent
- 2 to 3 years – 15 percent
- 3 to 4 years – 12 percent
- 4 to 6 years – 20 percent
- 6 to 8 years – 11 percent
- 8 to 10 years – 7 percent
- 10 to 20 years – 12 percent
- 20 years and over – 2 percent
- Life sentence – 18 percent

Almost one-half (46 percent) of inmates on snapshot day had a grade nine education or less, another 29 percent had grade ten or eleven, and 25 percent had grade twelve or higher. Forty-three percent of inmates were also unemployed at the time of incarceration. The majority of inmates (94 percent) were reported to be Canadian citizens. If 6 percent (832 people) of federal inmates did not have Canadian citizenship, why were they not deported? (Seventy-five percent of Canadians are in favour of deportation for committing a crime in Canada.)

Risk/needs data for inmates was supplied by CSC through the *Offender Management System (OMS)*. Need dimensions were assessed and they included:

- Employment problems
- Marital/family problems
- Social interaction
  (criminal or negative social associations)

- Attitude
  (e.g., unmotivated to change, pro-criminal values)
- Community functioning
  (e.g., lack of skills to manage life in the community)
- Personal/emotional problems
  (e.g., mental ability, sexual behaviour,
  cognitive skills)
- Substance abuse

In CSC, these inmates were classified according to three levels of risk (refers to the risk of re-offending) ranging from "low" to "high." The largest proportion of inmates was classified as high risk at 59 percent, while 34 percent were classified as medium risk, and 8 percent as low risk.

The same 1996 report details the distribution of risk broken down by offence type. The "high" risk of re-offending associated with federal inmates according to a particular offence is as follows:

Crimes against the Person

- Homicide/attempted murder – 80 percent
- Sexual assault – 68 percent
- Serious assault – 71 percent
- Minor assault – 66 percent
- Robbery – 52 percent
- Other violent offences – 71 percent

Property Crimes

- Break and enter – 47 percent
  (medium risk is at 47 percent)
- Theft – 35 percent (medium risk is at 49 percent)
- Fraud – 17 percent (medium risk is at 41 percent)
- Other property crimes – 43 percent
  (medium risk is at 47 percent)

Other Criminal Code/Federal Statutes

- Offensive weapons – 30 percent
  (medium risk is at 62 percent)
- Drugs – 20 percent (medium risk is at 48 percent)
- Impaired driving – 35 percent
  (medium risk is at 51 percent)
- Other *Criminal Code/Federal Statutes* – 29 percent
  (medium risk is at 44 percent)

The percentages in every category for "Crimes against the Person" are extremely high. This is a great cause for concern and provides a crystal clear picture: violent offenders *will* re-offend. The numbers speak for themselves. The "medium" risk statistics in their respective categories provide a very good indicator that these inmates will also re-offend.

Statistics for Adults in Provincial Correctional Institutions

In 2000/01 there was an average of 18,815 inmates incarcerated in provincial institutions. Of that number, 10,953 were sentenced offenders (already sentenced) and 7428 were remanded offenders (awaiting sentencing). Between 1978/79 and 2000/01, the counts of remanded offenders more than doubled.

Probation intakes (offenders who were sentenced to probation rather than prison) for the same year was reported at 81,939 and an average of 100,526 probationers were under the supervision of provincial probation services. From 1978/79 to 2000/01, probation counts have increased by 86 percent.

It seems as though almost all criminals are on probation. Crime obviously does pay, and not only that, it also sends a clear message that the courts see absolutely nothing wrong with that.

There are many unanswered questions that Canadians face: What do we do about prison overcrowding? How can we ease the burden of expenses associated with the imprisonment of criminals? How can we punish violent offenders and send a clear message? The federal government must search for acceptable solutions.

I believe that many Canadians will agree that it's time to build more prisons. The costs associated with building additional prisons will need to be addressed, and perhaps now is the time to begin implementing a system that forces criminals to monetarily assist in paying the costs associated with their rehabilitation.

Correctional user fees (fees charged to inmates who have been convicted of crimes for expenses such as programs and equipment (i.e.: ankle monitors)) are currently being used in many countries around the world, with notable success rates in the U.S. These fees are levied by correctional facilities and prison systems to assist in easing the financial burden associated with imprisonment.

I also believe it's time to seriously look at alternatives for punishing violent offenders, to perhaps consider the military-style training and/or rehabilitation concept called boot camps. Boot camps have been well established and are used in many countries in an effort to rehabilitate criminals.

Private prisons are one alternative to our current overcrowding concerns and should be considered, since the federal government has indicated that building more prisons is a very costly burden.

Private Prisons in Canada

Privatization refers to the transfer of traditional government responsibilities from the public sector to the private sector. Historically speaking, all prisons were private endeavours that came under the control of government. From a financial perspective, there are many points that would favour the privatization of prisons in Canada. The federal government must expand on the concept of privatization, or they must build new prisons and retain their responsibility.

During the last two decades, there has been a renewed interest from governments around the world to reconsider the usefulness of private prisons, and they are rapidly re-emerging. Canada is one country where they are beginning to emerge – the first private adult prison was opened in Penetanguishene, Ontario, in November, 2001.

Growing incarceration rates and increasing debt has caused some governments to look for new strategies in dealing with offenders. Many governments are questioning whether it can afford to house the current and/or anticipated offender population. Such questions need to be addressed in short order.

A brief summary and explanation of some of the issues is necessary in order for Canadians to have a better understanding of the options and how things have been implemented in the past – this includes increasing their knowledge of the system.

To begin, government correctional departments usually list the goals of corrections as incapacitation, punishment, deterrence and rehabilitation. When proceeding with privatization, specific constitutional concerns must be addressed to protect the rights of offenders in accordance with the *Canadian Charter of Rights and Freedoms.*

In Canada, the issue of overcrowding is one of the main concerns. The John Howard Society of Alberta (a non-profit agency concerned with the problems of crime and its prevention) issued a report in 2002 that indicates the Alberta government is considering private prison management. There are different categories of privatization in corrections and one of them is private prison industry, which involves the use of inmate labour for private purposes. These industries operate like public prison industries: inmates receive daily pay for their labour, and the goods and services produced are sold to the public.

There are opponents of privatization who argue that one reason government exists is to provide essential justice services. They believe that government has long been trusted with the authority to punish offenders and should therefore be extremely cautious in delegating this responsibility, as doing so may taint its position of trust in the public eye. Since government makes the laws, punishes offenders through the courts, and prisons are integral to government's punishment function, opponents believe it is wholly inappropriate for them to delegate its authority to punish to the private sector.

I believe that these opponents have just handed Canadians the very credible reasons we're looking for to support privatization – thank you for pointing out the failings of our existing government. Taking the Liberal Government's recent history into account, it's become evident that they wish to delegate their authority to punish to the private sector.

Our government says they can't afford to build new prisons for violent offenders. Now it looks like the privatization issue has provided them with the solution to this problem. The cost savings for government will now allow them to take these savings and provide funding for our dedicated frontline police officers, for new and improved equipment to assist them and much better resources to do their jobs.

The costs associated with operating correctional facilities are always a major concern. The potential for the private sector to reduce the expenses of incarceration is very high. Following are five main points put forward by proponents of privatization in support of their argument:

- The private sector is better equipped to finance, site and construct prisons swiftly and inexpensively.
- The private sector can create economies of scale by contracting across jurisdictions. For example, a prison in Alberta may be able to lower the costs to Alberta by contracting out unoccupied space for British Columbia or Saskatchewan.
- Private contracting greatly reduces public employee pensions and benefit plans while making use of more effective personnel management, better working conditions and less overcrowding.
- Privatization discourages waste and encourages innovation in material management without rigid procurement restrictions. Government normally dictates which suppliers can be used, procedures to be followed and what channels are appropriate to use.
- Government departments have a tendency to maximize their budgets to protect their long-term interests. The claim is that these departments try to enlarge their budgets in anticipation of later cutbacks – large budgets allow them to survive cutbacks without complete elimination.

Quality of service is another issue of concern. Supporters of privatization suggest that the private sector can create new levels of specialization and expertise, thereby increasing the quality of its services and promoting creativity and enthusiasm that is not possible by government.

A Hatry, Brounstein and Levinson (1993) study that compared private and public institutions in Kentucky and Massachusetts used several indicators to measure conditions. They concluded that privately operated facilities had a small advantage: By and large, both staff and inmates gave better ratings to the services and programs, escapee rates were lower, there were fewer disturbances by inmates, and speaking in general terms, staff and inmates felt more comfortable.

Evidently there are pros and cons to both sides of the issues. The debate can go on forever, but the time for debate is over. It's time for decision-making and implementing solutions. If there's already one private prison operating in Canada, then I see no reason to stop there. Can we really afford to continue debating these issues for the next five or ten years? I believe this country has waited long enough.

Correctional User Fees in Canada

Correctional user fees, or any fee that an offender is lawfully mandated to make that generates revenue for correctional purposes or that recovers all or a portion of the cost of services provided to an offender, have been in existence for hundreds of years. "Jailer's fees" date all the way back to eighteenth century England.

Today's correctional user fees exist in a variety of forms. Probation, electronic monitoring and parole supervision fees are widely used in the United States, and, in several states, they account for a significant portion of the cost of community-based supervision. These user fees are gaining popularity across North America and include fees for diversion programming as well as sanction-imposed programming. Program fees are typically the largest revenue generators (Parent, 1990). Examples of such programs are anger management, parenting, substance abuse and sex offender treatment programs, room and board fees and supervision fees for electronic monitoring, probation and parole. Correctional Services of Canada does not implement correctional user fees. It does, however, impose room and board fees on adult offenders both in prison and when released into the community. Canada's federal government prefers to spend thousands of taxpayers' money ($224.37 a day per federal inmate) on programs to make an inmate's life easier and help straighten them out.

According to a report issued by the John Howard Society of Alberta in 2001, in the state of Texas and thanks to aggressive legislation encouraging fee collection, the probation fees brought in $57 million – this equals more than one-half of that state's total probation supervision budget.

Canadians need to be fully aware that the federal government in Canada does not impose supervision fees on offenders. Parole supervision in the United States is entirely state-funded, and, other than post-secondary education, which is normally paid for by offenders (CSC, 2000), all programming available to offenders is also state-funded. Further, parolees receive five dollars per session for cognitive skills training, living skills programming and other core programming. The funds provided to parolees are considered "risk management;" they help ensure that offenders will attend.

Perks in Prison

Nicholas Chan was convicted in July 2004 of trafficking $7000 worth of heroin to an undercover police officer during a sting operation in 1999. In April 2005, as an inmate in the Calgary Remand Centre, Chan and his lawyer argued that remand centre conditions in Alberta have infringed on his rights. Chan complained that the three board games provided for the amusement of inmates were not enough and that his requests for amusements to satisfy his cultural differences were denied. He is "seeking a stay of his conviction" because of the conditions he is forced to live with.

Chan also complained that he was being deprived of physical contact with his family, who could only speak to him through a glass partition. Chan is also going to testify that he was forced to go on a hunger strike while on disciplinary segregation because his cell was monitored by a camera – he didn't want to suffer the indignity of being watched while he sat on the toilet to have a bowel movement.

If Mr. Chan is so traumatized by the conditions in prison here, why don't we present him with the opportunity to return to his country of origin under the International Transfer of Offenders program to serve out the remainder of his sentence? If Mr. Chan is a Canadian citizen, then I'm sure his lawyer will likely abuse the *Charter of Rights and Freedoms* to help his client accomplish his goals.

Prisoners in Canada are provided with almost all of the comforts of home: private two-bedroom units, three-day conjugal visits, colour TVs, cable, radios, libraries, computers, games rooms and gymnasiums. It costs Canadian taxpayers' $81,895.05 per year to feed and house a federal prisoner. That's more than an RCMP sergeant's salary (after twenty-five years of service) of just over $76,000.

Newspaper headlines hit hard in July, 2005: Corrections Canada (over the past three years) has issued 2170 passes on compassionate grounds for convicts to attend funerals or visit dying friends and relatives, at the expense of

Canadian taxpayers. Costs paid include flights (some first class), ground transportation, meals, escort services and overtime. It gets even worse: If convicts have the financial resources to foot the bill themselves, we pay for it anyway. Depending on destination and timing, convicts can either take a commercial flight or use an RCMP plane.

Hang on here. We have officers dying because of lack of resources, and the feds claim they don't have money to build more prisons, but we have money for this?

The same article also stated that security standards are dropped when prisoners are out on humanitarian passes, and escorts are often not equipped with weapons, restraints or pepper spray. Calgary Conservative MP Art Hangar said that Canadians should know how much of their tax dollars are being spent on inmates' trips: "I would suggest it's in the millions." In direct contrast, Hanger said that victims of violent crime are forced to pay their own way to attend events like parole hearings. "It's pathetic," he said.

Barb Hill, Director of Policy Development for The John Howard Society, claims to understand why some victims might be upset but that it's important to maintain a connection with family and the community. This is a slap in the face to victims and seems a direct contradiction of The John Howard Society of Canada's mission statement: "Effective, just and human responses to the causes and consequences of crime."

While this information was circulating through the media, there was another story that grabbed headlines: A young girl was raped and viciously attacked in Banff, Alberta, leaving her in a coma and near death. Her devastated family was hundreds of miles away in Ontario, trying desperately to find the financial resources to get to their daughter's hospital bedside. Numerous generous

Canadians stepped forward and opened their wallets. No RCMP plane was at the family's disposal.

It's clear that Canada's prison system needs an overhaul in the worst way. I'm partial to the now-famous "Tent City Jail" in Maricopa County, Arizona. An appropriate model of a boot camp, it opened on August 3, 1993, and has received worldwide media attention ever since. The jail houses over 2000 convicted men and women and is the brainstorm of one man: Maricopa County Sheriff Joe Apraio.

Sheriff Joe, "America's Toughest Sheriff," as he's been dubbed by the media, has over forty-two years of law enforcement experience. He's been elected for a second term with an 85 percent public approval rating. He's often said, "As Sheriff, I serve the public. The public is my boss." In serving the public, Sheriff Joe has implemented a number of unique policies, what he calls "get tough" policies.

He doesn't believe in coddling criminals or running jails like country clubs. He has banned smoking, coffee (it has no nutritional value), pornographic magazines, movies and unrestricted television in all of his county's jails. The cheapest meals in the country are served there at a cost of less than one dollar per meal. Chain gangs, male and female, work six days a week contributing thousands of dollars of free labour to the community. They clean the streets, paint over graffiti and bury the indigent in the county cemetery. Inmates have complained intensely about the conditions. Sheriff Joe responds, "This isn't the Ritz Carlton. If you don't like it, then don't come back."

At times, the temperature inside the tents can reach 138 degrees Fahrenheit or more.

Prisoners are sometimes given permission to strip down to their government-issued pink boxer shorts (they also have pink socks and towels). Inmates have complained that this treatment is inhumane. In true Sheriff Joe fashion, he says, "It's 120 degrees (Fahrenheit) in Iraq and our soldiers are living in tents too, and they have to wear full battle gear, but they didn't commit any crimes, so shut your darn mouth."

The Maricopa County Sheriff's Office was just plain old fed up with the system. It believes that criminals should be punished for their crimes, not live in luxury until they're paroled, only to go out and commit another crime. Sheriff Joe's philosophy of "zero tolerance" towards the criminal element has been embraced by his staff, deputies and the community alike.

There are numerous programs that are successfully managed out of this office. Operation Notification assists a business owner or operator in times of emergency through a coded number system. It's a valuable tool used to notify the business owner when their property has been illegally entered or damaged by fire, storm or vandalism.

Project Lifeline was established in 1997, and is a free cell phone program that provides victims of domestic violence and stalking with a cell phone that contains a pre-programmed emergency 911 number. The phones are donated by local companies and are distributed through-out the county to victims, who are allowed to keep their phone until he or she feels they are out of danger. The victim must complete an application form and sign an agreement not to reside with the abuser and to report to the program coordinator once a month.

The SMART (Shocking Mainstream Adolescents into Resisting Temptation) Tents Program is an innovative youth program designed to impress upon juveniles the truth about social standards and teaches students the real-ities of jail before they find out the hard way. They are bussed to the site after school on Friday and are met at the gate by the Sheriff's staff. The SMART Tent compound is located adjacent to Tent City and replicates the living conditions of the actual prisoners. Up to 140 students can sleep in the same tents, each containing ten bunk beds. They are given a tour of the adjacent facilities to show the actual living conditions of incarceration.

From that point on, they're treated just like the inmates – they change into black and white uniforms, eat jail food, sleep like the inmates and receive instruction on what prison life is all about. The staff on site teaches juvenile law, consequences and how to resist peer pressure and gang affiliation.

A new program has recently been implemented called S.T.A.R.S (Sheriff's Teaching Abuse Resistance to Students) and is strictly school-based with a principle objective of prevention. The program is based on teaching life skills. Juvenile delinquency serves as a gateway to criminal behaviour and it is vital to influence the perceptions of students about how society views alcohol, drugs, gangs and violence. Instructors are positive role models because of their experience and training in recognizing the signs and symptoms of problems like drug use, violent behaviour and gang activity.

The Sheriff's office also conducts an annual week long summer camp for children ages twelve and thirteen that live in the surrounding area. These children participate in a variety of activities from boating to horseback riding. It also heads up the war on drugs by taking the message to the streets with their new "tank" – a self-propelled Howitzer tank donated by the Department of Defense has been emblazoned with anti-drug messages and is being used as a tool to educate children of the dangers of drug abuse. The kids are given a program and video displays on the dangers involved with drugs.

The MASH (MCSO Animal Safe Hospice) program cares for abused and neglected animals that have been rescued by the Animal Cruelty Investigative Unit. The shelter provides a safe, healthy and healing home for these animals until they hopefully become adopted into loving, permanent homes. The housing facility was previously used to hold incarcerated inmates but was closed for repairs in 1999. No longer suitable for housing inmates, it was put to good use and now provides shelter for these animals. Detention officer staff and sentenced female inmates care for the animals and actively participate in their daily care and recovery. This also provides the inmates with useful learning skills when they are released from prison.

This example shows that there are options available. The system Canada currently has is insufficient to deal with the existing problems. In order to understand success or failure, attempts must be made in an effort to attain goals and seek positive solutions. The Liberal Government is apparently doing nothing – they do not appear to have any focus or sustainable and meaningful priority agenda.

Many of the programs Correctional Service Canada offers are worthwhile and necessary. Some others are not so necessary and are taking up much needed funding resources from other government-managed programs, like victim services. The Kingston Penitentiary in Kingston, Ontario, is a suitable example of waste in our prison system across the nation; it is also one of Canada's most famous penitentiaries.

The Kingston Penitentiary officially opened in 1835, under the reign of King William IV. It was British North America's first "penitentiary" and was officially called the "Provincial Penitentiary of the Province of Upper Canada," or the "Provincial Penitentiary" for short. Originally designed by American William Powers of Auburn, New York, the institution was heavily influenced by the system that had been established there. Mr. Powers was appointed the first Deputy Warden. In the aftermath of the 1971 riot, the penitentiary was re-designated as Ontario Region's Reception Centre, a role it served until 1981. Today it continues as a maximum-security institution, and as of April 6, 2004, it housed 494 inmates out of a capacity of 564.

Current programs available at the penitentiary:

Aboriginal Initiatives – A program mandated to create partnerships and strategies that enhance the safe and timely reintegration of Aboriginal offenders into the community.

Chaplain Services – Contracts for chaplaincy services are now being held with the following faith groups: Roman Catholic, Protestant, Jewish, Muslim, Sikh and Buddhist.

Community Forum Program – The CFP is designed to provide an opportunity for CSC and its partners to work together within a community to raise awareness and build a network of support to assist offenders. Organizations are eligible to receive up to a maximum of $5000 per forum under this program. The CFP will accept applications that clearly focus on building a network of community support to assist offenders in their reintegration efforts. Applications must address one of the following themes:

- The Needs of Offenders in the Community
- Enhancing the Role of Aboriginal Communities
- Healing and Re-integration
- Cultural Diversity
- Current Issues/Community Safety

CORCAN – Provides over two million hours of employment and training to federal offenders each year. Offenders work in businesslike settings where quality, value and productivity are key. CORCAN gives offenders the skills and attitudes needed when they return to society and become productive employees. The products and services they work on are sold to help pay for the cost of operating the program.

Correctional Programs – A structured intervention that addresses the factors directly linked to offenders' criminal behaviour. The purpose of the correctional system is to assist "the rehabilitation of offenders and their re-integration into the community as law-abiding citizens through the provision of programs in penitentiaries and in the community." Such programs include:

- Counter-Point Programs (for the prevention and treatment of criminal behaviour)
- Education and Employment
- Family Violence Programs
- Living Skills Programs
- Sexual Offender Programs
- Substance Abuse Programs
- Violence Prevention Programs

Ethno-cultural Issues – A major challenge to CSC is accommodating an offender population that is becoming more and more diverse. Community groups, agencies and representatives of CSC gathered in the city of Toronto, Ontario, March 11-13, 2005, to deal with this issue at the Building Bridges with Ethno-cultural Communities conference. Organized by Marcel Kabundi, Manager of Ethno-cultural Programs, his committee from the Reintegration Programs Division brought together people from over thirty countries for three days of stimulating presentations and discussion on how to raise awareness about cultural differences among staff and offenders and to establish helpful links for inmates to their communities.

International Transfer of Offenders – Canada has long cooperated in judicial and correctional matters. Transfer of Offenders Treaties enables offenders, with their explicit consent and with the discretionary approval of the sentencing country and of the country of citizenship, to serve their foreign-imposed sentence in their country of citizenship.

LifeLine – An innovative service provided through a partnership between CSC, National Parole Board and non-government organizations. It is about long-term offenders – lifers – who have successfully re-integrated into the community for at least five years and who are recruited to help other lifers throughout their sentences. LifeLine's mission is "to provide, through both the in-reach and the community component, an opportunity to motivate inmates and to marshal resources to achieve successful, supervised, gradual integration into the community."

In addition to this, on September 25, 2002, the official opening of the LifeLine Resource Centre in the Ministry of the Solicitor General Library took place. The LifeLine Resource Centre, through its collection of highly specialized materials on the LifeLine Concept, long-term incarceration and long-term offenders, will help facilitate CSC's work with lifers. There is now a broader range of tools at their disposal to assist them in better understanding the needs, experiences and potential contributions of this distinct population, and to plan for their safe re-entry into Canadian society.

Offender Management System (OMS) Renewal – The OMS is a computerized case file management system used by CSC, the National Parole Board and other criminal justice partners to manage information on federal offenders throughout their sentences. The system gathers, stores and retrieves information required for tracking offenders and for making decisions concerning their cases. Information on provincial offenders applying for parole in provinces without parole boards is also stored in OMS.

Programs for Families of Offenders – The aim of the "Private Family Visiting Program" is to enable inmates to develop and maintain positive family and community relationships that will assist them in preparing for reintegration into society as law-abiding citizens. Under the program, private family visits are allowed once every two months for periods of up to seventy-two hours per inmate. The actual frequency and duration of visits, however, are determined by the number of inmates participating in the program and the facilities available at the institution.

Visits take place in special family visiting units located within the institutional reserve in an area that provides as much privacy as reasonably possible. The fully furnished units have at least two bedrooms, a living room, kitchen and bathroom. Inmates are eligible for private family visiting except those inmates who are assessed as being currently at risk of becoming involved in family violence, in receipt of "Unescorted Temporary Absences" for the purpose of contact with family members, or in a Special Handling Unit or awaiting a decision or have been approved for transfer to a Special Handling Unit. Family members eligible to participate in the program are spouses, common-law partners, children, parents, foster-parents, siblings, grandparents and persons with whom, in the opinion of the institutional head, the inmate has a close familial bond.

It is up to individual Canadians to decide for themselves how they feel about the programs, not just in the Kingston Penitentiary, but all federal, provincial/territorial correctional institutions as well, all of which have programs in place for the inmates and their families.

Restorative Justice – An approach to justice that focuses on repairing the harm caused by crime while holding the offender responsible for his or her actions, by providing an opportunity for the parties directly affected by a crime –

victim(s), offender and community – to identify and address their needs in the aftermath of a crime and seek a resolution that affords healing, reparation and reintegration, and prevents future harm. In Canada, mediators or facilitators assist accused persons and their families to meet with victims, police and others to discuss and resolve the incident.

These processes are rapidly being adopted within Canada as well as internationally, as a way of responding to crime and victimization. However, there is little information quantifying the use of these programs and services in criminal matters in Canada.

Many of the concepts in restorative justice philosophy find their origins in the traditional practices of indigenous cultures around the world (Achtenberg, 2000). According to the philosophy, criminal behaviour is primarily caused by the alienation of certain members from society at large. Accordingly, when a person becomes alienated or disconnected from society, it is considered to be the responsibility of everyone in that society to bring the person back into a harmonious relationship with him or her "self," as well as with the rest of the community (Achtenberg, 2000).

Canadian Aboriginal practices are based on the use of "circles" – sentencing, healing and releasing circles. This practice involves having communities, families, elders and disputants meet to discuss and resolve issues. Participants sit in a circle and may pass a "talking stick" or "talking feather" to each speaker. In addition, traditional Aboriginal ceremonies such as burning sweet grass, passing a tobacco pipe or entering sweat lodges often accompany circles.

Amendments to the *Criminal Code* came into effect in September 1996, to reflect the preference for sentences other than incarceration, especially in certain cases. Specifically, Section 718.2 (e) of the *Criminal Code of Canada* requires a court to consider the following principle: that "all available sanctions other than imprisonment that are reasonable in the circumstances, should be considered for all offenders, with particular attention to the circumstances of Aboriginal offenders."

In 2003, an on-line consultation was held regarding Department of Justice documents discussing the values, principles and guidelines for restorative justice. Twenty-three responses to the consultation were received and some recommendations were made involving complete consultation with the Aboriginal community and three survey options ranging in cost between $120,000 and $180,000 to take an inventory of all funded (government or otherwise) and/or un-funded restorative justice programs.

The federal government requested a special study be conducted by the *Canadian Centre for Justice Statistics* that would produce an inventory of restorative justice programs and services in criminal matters. This study was not intended to examine the effectiveness of the programs and services or to provide an audit of program and service delivery. Therefore, this study neither examines outcomes in terms of success, or how or if resolutions are achieved or satisfied.

The restorative justice process seems to be used quite widely and frequently across Canada, but no one knows if it works or is accomplishing anything. The government has put thousands of dollars into the program to take an inventory but have indicated they're not interested in the success or failure of the programs or whether resolutions are achieved. Common logic dictates that if you're going to buy a car, you better make sure it works first.

Correctional Service Canada has also established programs for women in prison:

Women Offender Programs and Issues – There are a vast range of additional programs and services that are available at CSC's new institutions for women that play a significant role in the successful reintegration of women offenders. For example:

- Living Skills Program
- Substance Abuse Programs
- Literacy and Continuous Learning Programs
- Survivors of Abuse and Trauma Programs
- Mother-child Program
- Other Programs and Services

The development and implementation of these additional programs are the responsibility of the individual institutions and regions. They include multicultural, recreation and leisure, vocational and educational, peer support team, and health programs and services (both educational and intervention programs).

Victim Services in Canada

In 1988, Canada established the Canadian Statement of Basic Principles of Justice for Victims of Crime. These basic principles were "intended to ensure fair treatment and inclusion of victims and to guide federal/provincial/territorial laws, policies and procedures which are the means to implement these principles." It was based on the 1985 UN Declaration of Basic Principles for Victims of Crime and Abuse of Power. In 1989, CSC committed itself "to ensure that the concerns of victims are taken into account in discharging our responsibilities."

The Canadian Statement of Basic Principles of Justice for Victims of Crime states the following:

1. Victims should be treated with courtesy, compassion and respect for their dignity and

privacy and should suffer the minimum of necessary inconvenience from their involvement with the criminal justice system.

2. Victims should receive, through formal and informal procedures, prompt and fair redress for the harm which they have suffered.

3. Information regarding remedies and the mechanisms to obtain them should be made available to victims.

4. Information should be made available to victims about their participation in criminal proceedings and the scheduling, progress and ultimate disposition of the proceedings.

5. Where appropriate, the view and concerns of victims should be ascertained and assistance provided throughout the criminal process.

6. Where the personal interests of the victim are affected, the views or concerns of the victim should be brought to the attention of the court, where appropriate and consistent with criminal law and procedure.

7. Measures should be taken when necessary to ensure the safety of victims and their families and to protect them from intimidation and retaliation.

8. Enhanced training should be made available to sensitize criminal justice personnel to the needs and concerns of victims and guidelines developed, where appropriate, for this purpose.

9. Victims should be informed of the availability of health and social services and other relevant assistance so that they might continue to receive the necessary medical, psychological and social assistance through existing programs and services.

10. Victims should report the crime and cooperate with the law enforcement authorities.

In 1992, the Canadian government established the *Corrections and Conditional Release Act* that officially gave victims certain rights, primary of which was to receive certain information about offenders as they served out their sentence. Changes to this legislation are currently being considered; for example, the right to make a statement at parole board hearings and/or access audiotapes of those hearings.

All operational units within the CSC, including both institutions and parole offices, presently have a "Victim Liaison Coordinator" to ensure that information about offenders is shared in a timely and professional manner with victims. Both CSC and the National Parole Board collaborate in the delivery of information to victims.

CSC is currently involved in an "intensive review of its services to victims." It is in the process of finalizing its Standard Operating Practices and Commissioner's Directives concerning victim notification in consultation with both internal and external partners including victims' rights groups. The training of staff is recognized as a priority, as is the security of personal victim information, timely notification and doing everything possible to prevent secondary re-victimization. These efforts are being made within a restorative justice framework that recognizes the importance of victims in the aftermath of crime.

I can only guess that this "intensive review" is taking place because of the horrible failure of our system to properly protect and notify the victims of crime when there have been changes involving the person who was convicted of committing a violent crime against them. There is a serious lack of support and protection when it comes to the victims of violent crime. My own first-hand knowledge and personal experience as a victim of a violent crime just adds credence to the fact that there are serious flaws and issues when it comes to the rights of the victims.

Currently, very little is known about the services available to victims and the people who use them. To date, the only source of national data on services for victims is a *Statistics Canada* survey that collects information on services for abused women and children – a much needed information source.

To begin addressing the lack of information regarding the various types of victim services, a national voluntary survey was conducted for the first time in 2002/03 through the *Canadian Centre for Justice Statistics*. It revealed that between April 1, 2002, and March 31, 2003, a total of 412 agencies reported serving 359,767 clients that were using victim services. In a "snapshot" taken on October 22, 2003, a total of 373 agencies in Canada reported serving 4358 clients on that day. A breakdown of the information was recorded and reported as follows:

- 77 percent (3372) were female victims, 23 percent (986) were male victims.
- 78 percent (3421) were victims of crimes against the person:
  - 38 percent were victims of sexual assault
  - 4 percent were victims of criminal harassment
  - 2 percent were secondary victims of homicide
  - 3 percent were secondary victims of other crimes resulting in the loss of life
  - 52 percent were victims of other violent offences, including physical assault.
- Of the 1300 victims of sexual assault
  - 16 percent were victimized by a spouse, ex-spouse or intimate partner
  - 45 percent were victimized by other family members
  - 39 percent were victimized by others.
- Of the 1780 victims of other violent offences

- 68 percent were victimized by a spouse, ex-spouse or intimate partner
- 11 percent were victimized by other family members
- 21 percent were victimized by others.
• On snapshot day, the reporting agencies provided services to clients as follows:
  - 45 percent received emotional support
  - 39 percent received general information
  - 28 percent received case/trial updates
  - 26 percent received information on the criminal justice system structure and process
  - 23 percent received education, prevention or training
  - 22 percent received court information.

These statistics reveal a couple of different things. All of the victims were attending victim services for the same reason; someone had violently and physically assaulted them. Most of the victims were also seeking emotional support and information because they were violated. The average number of victims each agency attended to was twelve. It is very evident that the need for these services is great. If our government spent adequate money supporting the victims instead of pampering the prisoners, I believe we'd have fewer victims on our hands.

In terms of events that impacted the delivery of service, agencies frequently made reference to funding and changes in federal legislation. In some cases, these changes have caused an increased workload and shortage of staff. The impacts of changes in funding were a shortage of staff or volunteers and longer waiting times for services. The one commonality with almost every agency reporting was this: The biggest challenges they will face in the coming year are funding problems, possible budget cuts, shortages of permanent staff and volunteers and an increased workload because of legislative changes.

Agencies indicated they will be putting more pressure on government funding, will try to recruit additional volunteers, prioritize clients and case loads and raise awareness among the RCMP of the services they offer.

Why is it that criminals are encouraged to use such a vast array of services right on their doorstep, while victim agencies have to struggle to survive and be heard? In 2004/05, Alberta Solicitor General Harvey Cenaiko announced that the provincial government had doled out $3.2 million in grants to eighty-nine victim-serving community organizations. Mr. Cenaiko said, "Victims of crime need to know that the government listened when they told us that more support was needed."

This money amounts to just under $36,000 per agency for the year and is barely enough to pay for the average salary of one full-time employee, let alone provide services. This was a 61 percent increase over the previous year, so essentially this means they were getting nothing before. Canadians should also know that these grants are exclusively funded by the federal and provincial surcharges collected from offenders. This is absolutely proof positive that victims are ignored in this country.

Hopefully now, a much clearer picture has been provided to all Canadians with what is, or isn't, happening within our federal and territorial/provincial prison system. There is much work to be done and the federal government needs to get at it. If we continue to let the system run amuck the way it currently is, then we will continue to have a system that isn't working to its potential in protecting Canadians. There are many ways to effectively save money, spend money effectively and get the job done. The millions of taxpayers' dollars being wasted by a system that caters to criminals is embarrassing. As for the prisoners in Canada, our government has allowed them to abuse the system for far too long, and it needs to stop. The victims in this country are being ignored and society must participate in stopping these injustices from continuing along its path of destruction. We all deserve better.

The parole boards, sentencing and legislation are clearly not reflecting the needs and wants of Canadians. Victims of violent crime in this country should no longer be forced to tolerate the negligence of a system that is the responsibility of our government and is failing in almost every aspect thus far. It's time for the government to repair the damage being inflicted on this country. If it doesn't start now, what will happen five or six years from now?

Chapter 6 – Canada's Young Offenders

"The solution of adult problems tomorrow

depends in large measure upon the way

our children grow up today. There is no greater

insight into the future than recognizing that,

when we save children, we save ourselves."

Margaret Mead

"It used to be believed that the parent had unlimited

claims on the child and rights over him.

In a truer view of the matter, we are coming to see

that the rights are on the side of the child and

the duties on the side of the parent."

William G. Sumner

Parents want the best for their children. They work hard at their chosen careers to provide all the comforts and luxuries money can buy, sometimes at great personal sacrifice. They encourage their children to express their opinions, to be individuals and make their own mark in life. Then there are those parents who are neglectful, abusive, or merely absent. Most of these children do whatever is necessary to survive. They may be grateful or resentful to make it through another day, to live long enough to make something of their lives.

There have been many studies and much research that has gone into the struggles and problems regarding Canada's youth. Family violence against children and youth is a very critical factor in what's happening with our young people today. Some statistics will tell you that youth crime is decreasing; others will agree but attest to the fact that our youth are also becoming increasingly more violent in their crimes. I believe, as a nation, we are not dealing with that aspect accordingly.

In 2002, according to a subset of ninety-four police departments representing 56 percent of the national volume of crime, approximately 27 percent of all violent crimes were victims of family violence. Children under the age of eighteen accounted for 61 percent of victims of sexual assault and 20 percent of all victims of physical assault. The rates of physical assaults against children increased with age, and witnessing violence in the home has been linked to short and long-term behaviour problems such as overt aggression (fighting, making threats, anger, bullying) and emotional problems. Between 1993 and 2002, over two-thirds of homicides involving children and youth were committed by a family member.

Punishment in these cases is even more difficult to comprehend: results from linked police and court records from 1997/98 to 2000/01 indicate the most common sanction for family violence was *probation* and occurred in 71 percent of cases of violence against children and youth. For the same period, family members convicted of sexual assault against children and youth were more likely to receive a "conditional sentence" – approximately 24 percent versus 15 percent for a non-family member. How can our justice system hand out such lenient sentences for family members? This type of sentencing goes directly against the very moral fiber of this country. Family members are in a position of trust, and the penalties must be severe for breaching that trust. The message to our children is pretty clear: it's not okay for a stranger to beat me, but it's okay if mom or dad beats me. These children are our future, and if our courts don't start sending a message defending these children, how can we possibly expect any better from them?

Violence is violence. It shouldn't matter if the perpetrator is a stranger or a family member. These problems need to be dealt with swiftly and severely. Family-related sexual and physical assaults for both boys and girls reached their highest levels in 2002. Speaking directly to domestic violence, the majority of accused (58 percent) had a criminal record for another violent offence. These children have nowhere to turn. If our government and the justice system don't get serious about this, we're going to have more dead children on our hands.

The intense suffering of these children is enough to make your heart stop. Their bodies are bruised and their minds are crippled. What their perpetrators have done to them has life-long negative effects. Some heal, recover and go on to live a good and decent life. Others do not. They go on to, consciously or not, model their abuser's behaviour and become abusers themselves. This is the flip side of youth justice. James Roszko abused a boy over a seven-year period and spent two-and-a-half years in jail. That is not justice.

In 1908, Canada's Parliament passed the Juvenile Delinquents Act, which was replaced in 1982 with the *Young Offenders Act*. Much criticism followed. Opinion was divided between those that believed it was too lenient and those that believed it was too harsh. As a result, the Act lost credibility with the public and failed to correct the systematic problems in the youth justice system. The government attempted to restore some credibility by introducing amendments in 1986, 1992 and 1995.

By the late 1990s, it was realized that these amendments failed. In 1998, the federal government announced a new strategy for youth justice. In February, 2002, Parliament passed the *Youth Criminal Justice Act* to replace the *Young Offenders Act*. It became effective in April, 2003. The goals of the new act place emphasis on the rehabilitation and re-entry of a young offender into society. Criticism from the public cited that the youth justice system lacked a clear philosophy, and because of that, a *Declaration of Principles* was implemented. The youth criminal justice system was given guidelines that were set out to address the underlying circumstances of a young person's offending behaviour, rehabilitate young persons who commit offences, reintegrate them into society and ensure that a young person is subject to meaningful consequences for his or her offences in order to promote the long-term protection of the public.

Youth crime statistics may surprise many Canadians. Violent crimes are rampant, as are property crimes. And it isn't just males committing these crimes. In 2003, the following serious police-reported crimes were charged against children considered to be "young offenders" between the ages of twelve and seventeen:

Violent Crimes

- 56 homicides (47 boys charged, 9 girls charged)
- 69 attempted murders (57 boys, 12 girls)
- 1450 sexual assaults (1409 boys, 41 girls)
- 133 other sexual offences (127 boys, 6 girls)
- 15,828 non-sexual assaults (10,976 boys, 4852 girls)
- 1 abduction (1 boy)
- 3127 robberies (653 boys, 474 girls)

Total = 20,664

Property Crimes

- 11,158 for breaking and entering
  (10,016 boys, 1142 girls)
- 4949 for motor vehicle thefts (4153 boys, 796 girls)
- 284 for theft over $5000 (239 boys, 45 girls)
- 12,307 for theft of $5000 and under
  (8477 boys, 3830 girls)
- 4985 for possession of stolen property
  (3897 boys, 1088 girls)
- 35,092 for fraud (27,719 boys, 7373 girls)

Total = 68,775

Other Crimes

- 40 for prostitution (7 boys, 33 girls)
- 1506 for offensive weapons (1380 boys, 126 girls)
- 576 for arson (497 boys, 79 girls)
- 11,190 for bail violations (8174 boys, 3016 girls)
- 15,129 for other *Criminal Code* offences excluding traffic (12,222 boys, 2907 girls)

Total = 28,441

Drugs (possession, trafficking and importation)

- 19 for heroin (15 boys, 4 girls)
- 500 for cocaine (373 boys, 127 girls)
- 4463 for cannabis (3924 boys, 539 girls)
- 551 for other drugs (453 boys, 98 girls)

Total = 5533

Other *Federal Statutes*

- 92 for the *Canada Shipping Act* (71 boys, 21 girls)
- 1 for the *Customs Act* (1 boy)
- 3 for the *Excise Act* (3 boys)
- 13 for the *Immigration Act* (9 boys, 4 girls)
- 4 for the *Firearms Act* (4 boys)
- 5057 listed as other *Federal Statutes* (3603 boys, 1454 girls)

Total = 5170

Youth crime is not being committed by a specific category of young persons. Some of these youth have grown up in abusive homes, some are from middle and upper class families, some are supporting their addictions, some are doing it for money, some have nothing better to do and some are bowing to peer pressure. Punishment for these children depends on their particular situation. Some require a hard-line view and others require a more sympathetic view.

A great many people and organizations in Canada believe that society is best protected through rehabilitation of young offenders, that rehabilitation is necessary if we are to expect these children to become law-abiding, contributing members of society.

Rehabilitation – that's a tough nut to crack. Statistics will offer both positive and negative results on both ends of the spectrum. Just because it works for one young offender, doesn't necessarily mean it will work for the next. A disturbed young person who has been raised in an abusive family needs counseling, patience, understanding and someone they can trust. A functional child bowing to peer pressure or the want of material gain may need a reality check – perhaps some time spent in a boot camp facility to learn some new skills and respect for others. Children with addiction problems will require addiction treatment and on-going support systems. Increased federal funding is required in order to address the needs of society, and these young people are a part of this society.

The Canadian public may not know that, in many cases, organized crime members and gangs use children to do their dirty work. They recruit, abuse and bribe children to steal cars, prostitute themselves, deliver and pick up drugs, anything that allows them to reap the rewards and stay out of jail. Children are more willing to take these risks knowing that the punishment will not be severe, and of course, money is the greatest motivator. This is a sensitive topic and again alludes to the courts' ability or inability to define and distinguish between youth who are in serious need of treatment or counseling and those that are committing crime in order to make a quick buck.

Recent statistics for the year 2001/02 show that sixteen year olds accounted for 30 percent of drug cases and seventeen year olds accounted for 39 percent. Accused persons aged fifteen appeared in 18 percent of all drug cases, while those aged twelve, thirteen and fourteen showed proportionately less involvement, accounting for 1 percent, 3 percent and 9 percent respectively. In youth court for the same year, probation was the most frequently assigned sanction in 83 percent of convicted trafficking cases and 56 percent of convicted possession cases. In total for drug trafficking and possession convictions, 11 percent were sentenced to custody (secure and open), 66 percent were sentenced to probation and 17 percent were fined. Secure custody facilities are for youth who the courts have deemed as requiring close monitoring and/or programming in a confined setting. Open custody residences are operated by agencies under contract to the ministry and provide residential supervision within the community.

Why children offend and what can be done about it is a slippery slope. Opinions vary, but I believe the root of the problem lies with the parents, more often than not. Parents often don't know where their children are, who they're with or what they're doing. Many could be said to be suffering from every parent's best friend: denial. It's time for parents to be held responsible for the actions of their children until they reach the age of eighteen years. If their child is arrested for vandalism, shoplifting or stealing a car, then the parents should pay restitution. If the law was changed to this effect, I believe that the number of young offenders in this country would be drastically reduced. Parents would change their attitudes and the way they handle their children's criminal activity.

Today's youth are different from the youth of thirty years ago. Too often, juvenile delinquents are assumed to be the anti-social type, perhaps with long hair, a tattoo or a piercing. No longer. Children from stable, middle-class, two-parent families are committing serious and violent crimes. It's happening in every demographic, no matter race, colour or socio-economic background.

In my day, if we found ourselves in trouble with the law, it was a very serious issue and it was dealt with accordingly. For the most part, parents made it their responsibility to make amends for any ill will that may have been caused by their children's lack of judgment. That was the right thing to do, and they did it. We had to face the music, listen to the lectures about how we should thank our lucky stars and the heavens above that no one was injured or killed because of our bad decision. Our parents weren't above letting us spend a night in jail either. In all our teenage rebellion, there was still respect for authority.

It seems that many of today's parents prefer to blame someone else for their child's unacceptable behaviour and actions. The excuses are endless: they were hanging around with a bad crowd, they were provoked or they couldn't possibly be involved. Their denial will convince them that their child is innocent and will therefore be treated as such. How will today's children learn anything in this life if parents continue to come to their rescue every time they break the law?

Parents also need to check their own behaviour. How often have parents told their children not to drink and drive, only to do the exact opposite and drive home after consuming three, five or ten cocktails, with their children in the car no less? Or how often have parents been stopped for a speeding ticket and then cursed the officer in front of their children? How many parents lecture their children on drug abuse and then turn around and pop a valium? Children are observant. They learn from this hypocrisy. Parents should hang their heads in shame for not practicing what they preach. It is very clear some parents have failed miserably when it comes to morally and ethically rearing their children.

A good deal of the blame also has to fall in the lap of Canada's lawmakers, who insist that children under the age of twelve are not capable of knowing the difference between right and wrong, and, therefore, should not be held accountable for their actions. My son was in the second grade and only seven years old when he berated me for not putting my seatbelt on. He knew full well that it was against the law. So please don't tell me that children don't know the difference between right and wrong. If they're smart enough to wear a bigger, roomier jacket to the shopping mall with the intent of shoplifting, then they're smart enough to know that what they're doing is wrong and punishable by law. We don't give our children enough credit, and sometimes they're a lot smarter than we are.

Many Albertans will remember the Taber school shooting in 1999. A fourteen-year-old boy opened fire in his high school with a sawed-off shotgun, killing a sixteen-year-old student and wounding another. He was sentenced to a ten-year conditional sentence, three years of which was to be served in prison. A conditional sentence is given to less serious offenders who will not endanger the safety of the public. So, murder isn't a serious offence? The public isn't in danger? Pending the decision to transfer this youth to a correction residence, Dr. Lisa Ramshaw told a court that this school shooter demonstrated psychopathic tendencies, that "there was no overall change" in his diagnosis and he remains a "significant risk to the public."

On August 15, 2005, the school shooter, now twenty, now identified as Todd Cameron Smith, made headlines again. He escaped custody from a halfway house in Toronto and was unlawfully at large. On August 16, Mr. Smith was back in custody without incident.

Situations like this are a kick in the behind to every law-abiding Canadian citizen. These meagre sentences are nothing more than a slap on the fingers. The thing I believe upsets Canadians the most is that the legislation is being abused by the system itself. How did a court over-look the clear definition of "conditional sentence"?

The bottom line is that we must get tougher with our children, and the law must get tougher with our children. How many times have you heard from troubled teenagers that they shoplift, drink or get involved with drugs because they're trying to get their parents to pay attention? Many of them end up in trouble because they don't believe anyone cares about them or their parents don't have time for them. By the time some of these kids reach the age of twelve or thirteen, things have spun out of control, and, by that time, it may be too late.

Take the case of Turner Valley RCMP officer Tom Christie. While off duty and out for a bike ride, a sixteen and a seventeen year old knocked him to the ground and beat him unconscious. He was struck at least fifty times to the head and body, and spent six days in hospital. He now suffers from headaches, memory problems and fatigue. What prompted the attack? Constable Christie had asked the boys to pick up some empty beer cans they tossed in an alley near his home.

In court, one of the boys showed little emotion but said, "I'm sorry about what happened. I saw my friend in a fight and I was kinda drunk and I jumped in." The youth court judge presiding over the case sentenced the youth to an eleven-month sentence, two-thirds of which will be spent behind bars before he is allowed to serve the balance of the sentence under community supervision.

Where were the parents?

Correctional Juvenile Boot Camps in Canada

Juvenile boot camps are correctional programs for delinquent youth in a military-style environment. These programs typically emphasize discipline and physical conditioning and were developed as a rigorous alternative to longer terms of confinement in juvenile correctional facilities. Many, but not all, of these programs are followed by a period of probation or some form of aftercare. Boot camps are generally restricted to non-violent or first-time offenders.

Despite all of the issues and concerns regarding boot camps for young offenders, there are programs that opened in three provinces, but the information is very limited. These camps/programs are listed below.

Alberta's Shunda Creek Youth Correction Camp

In January 1993, this facility was opened for the young offenders in Alberta (Alberta Justice, 1993). This camp operates year round and is directed at repeat young offenders serving at least a three-month sentence. The camp employs eight correctional staff members, a substance abuse counsellor, a psychologist, a life skills trainer and an Aboriginal program coordinator (Alberta Justice, 1993).

The work camp combines counselling/education and work programs to help young offenders develop a strong work ethic and life skills which are necessary to meet the demands of responsible living in the future (Alberta Justice, 1993). The work program emphasizes physical fitness through manual labour. Some of the work projects include brush cleaning, wood chopping, construction, campsite maintenance and trail maintenance. The counselling/educational components teach life skills, employment search techniques, anger management, cultural awareness (specifically for Aboriginals) and substance abuse issues.

Currently, there is no follow-up data concerning recidivism rates of Shunda Creek participants (Personal Communication, Alberta Justice staff member, July 1997).

Alberta's Aboriginal Young Offender Corrections Camp

This corrections camp is an open custody work camp that combines educational programs with culturally specific programs (Alberta Justice, 1995). This program addresses issues of concern and importance to Aboriginal people. According to Mike Cardinal, the former minister responsible for Aboriginal programs, the "Aboriginal young offender camp is significant because it's the first of its kind in this province and represents the dedicated efforts of the Bigstone Cree First Nation, Alberta Justice and Aboriginal Affairs" (Cardinal, as cited in Alberta Justice, 1995).

Ontario's Project Turnaround

Ontario's first boot camp opened in Medonte Township in July, 1997. The program employs approximately forty staff members, including clinicians, youth workers, drill instructors and administrative staff (Company selected..., 1997). The program accommodates thirty-two male juvenile repeat offenders who have received a youth court disposition of open custody or probation following a custodial sentence (Company selected, 1997).

Project Turnaround is a highly regimented, sixteen-hour-a-day program. The project addresses issues such as academics, life skills, literacy training and problem solving techniques, but the main focus of the program is on physical fitness and hard work (Company selected..., 1997). Project Turnaround mirrors a strict military way of life and models boot camps in the United States.

Secure Custody Facilities in Manitoba

In September, 1994, the Manitoba government and Department of Corrections transformed existing policies regarding young offenders committed to secure custody facilities. Under the new model, all young offenders in secure custody participate in programs and lifestyles that closely resemble the structure of boot camps. This model focuses on "rigorous confinement, austere conditions, defined expectations and consequences and highly structured activities" (Hill, 1996, p. 2).

Young offenders in all secure custody facilities are expected to participate in education and exercise programs. The education programs focus on developing the young persons' interpersonal and problem solving skills as well as literacy and other academic skills. The exercise routine focuses on physical training for overall personal health (Personal Communication, Community Youth Corrections staff member, July 1997).

Proponents argue that Manitoba has undergone a positive transformation in the way it deals with its young offenders. Others, on the other hand, argue that Manitoba has created a boot camp atmosphere in secure custody facilities because they now adhere to strict and disciplined schedules in which young offenders are provided with only the basic necessities and must follow monotonous regimented routines.

Although Manitoba has not adopted a "true" militaristic atmosphere that is common to Ontario's Project Turnaround and other boot camps in the United States, it still promotes an atmosphere of strict authoritarian discipline.

In Alberta, there is a common perception that offenders are "getting off easy." As a result of the public outcry for more punitive measures for criminals (adult and youth), the use of shock incarceration (boot camps) is seen as introducing these punitive measures. There are several factors that frustrate the use of defined boot camps in Alberta, making their "truly defined" use currently unacceptable.

First, Canadian legislation does not currently allow for significantly shorter sentences based on the successful completion of any program. Rather, prison sentences in Canada are automatically reduced by one-third. This legislation prevents Canada from implementing the use of boot camps in a more concrete manner. The system can and will work if our government does something about it.

Second, forced participation in the program would be far less likely to succeed in rehabilitating the offender. Motivation is a big factor that allows boot camps to instill change in their participants. Without the option of shorter sentences (e.g., 220 days in a correctional facility versus 90 days in boot camp), it is unlikely the offender will be willing to contribute positively to the experience. Offenders would have a choice, but they must graduate from boot camp in order to cancel out what would have been a 220-day sentence.

Third, punishment alone does not work as a motivating factor in changing an offender's behaviour. The incorporation of other programs like drug counseling, employment counseling and education would have to become part of the curriculum in order to have a successful formula.

In Canada, a number of conditions would be necessary if boot camps with a more meaningful programming system were to be successful:

- All participants would have to be diverted from prison, not probation.
- There must be enough participants to ensure a significant decrease in the prison population.
- Most of the participants would have to successfully complete the program.

- Sentences would have to be reduced in exchange for boot camp participation.
- The program would have to have rehabilitative value.

The Canadian government needs to seriously consider this option in a more concrete manner – this would be the much needed replacement or alternative program for our existing "extra-judicial sanctions/alternative measures program" or some of the "restorative justice programs" that are currently lacking the teeth required to accomplish much of anything when it comes to young offenders.

Admission and eligibility requirements must be met and approved by the courts. The boot camps are set up for short-term stays covering periods of approximately 90 to 180 days. Their day starts at 5:30 a.m. and ends at 9:30 p.m. and is completed with physical training, labour, drill exercises, educational programs, counseling and support sessions that enable them to work through their problems and difficulties in a non-destructive manner.

The four predominant boot camp goals are to:

- create a less expensive alternative to prison,
- reduce recidivism (a falling back or relapse into prior criminal habits, especially after conviction and punishment) and promote successful reintegration of the offender into the community,
- deter crime and promote community relations,
- improve control and management techniques.

Boot camp prisons impose a harsh and demanding regime on offenders. Offenders either volunteer or are required to complete a short-term stay. Usually offenders voluntarily opt into the more intense short-term program rather than accept a longer prison sentence. Judges and corrections officials, however, make the final decision, and most programs are limited to first-time felony offenders only. Over half of the programs allow violent offenders to participate.

Many people in Canada will be up in arms over this topic. My research indicates that this option is being readily used in the Unites States, and with huge success. If the government seriously implements the necessary changes in legislation with respect to young offenders, I believe we will have a system that works well – one that actually sees some serious results.

If you weigh the pros and cons of boot camps and compare them to Canada's current system, the choice becomes very clear. Much of the data supporting juvenile boot camps is hard to argue with, and it could save Canadian taxpayers a substantial amount of money compared to the existing costs.

Canadians would finally have a system containing a preventative tool that is combined with a delinquency corrector. The main focus of these camps is simply "training" using the military-style regime. Studies have shown a lower recidivism (re-offence) rate among boot camp graduates. The success is attributed to rehabilitative programming and quality after-care. There are groups that oppose juvenile boot camps and will provide varying statistics.

Since their creation in 1983 in the United States, boot camps have developed and changed considerably. More recently there has been an incorporation of education, counseling or vocational training. Once offenders have completed their terms at boot camp, they are released under intense community supervision. Most states have post-release programs, which include work programs, employment counseling, drug counseling and daily therapeutic community meetings to assist in the offender's reintegration into society. Thirteen nation-wide programs have developed aftercare models specifically for boot camps.

Boot Camps in the United States

In the United States, the differences between boot camps and regular adult prisons are evident in the following account of a typical boot camp:

> Upon arrival at boot camp prisons, male inmates have their heads shaved (females are permitted short haircuts) and are informed of the strict program rules. The ten- to sixteen-hour day begins with a pre-dawn march to an exercise yard for one or two hours of physical training and drill. They march to breakfast and to work sites, where they participate in hard physical labour. They then march back to the compound, where they participate in more exercise and drill. Dinner is followed by evening programs that include counseling, life skills training, academic education, and/or drug education and treatment. Inmates generally earn privileges. Those who successfully complete the program attend an elaborate graduation ceremony with visitors and family invited to attend. Awards are sometimes presented to acknowledge progress made during the program (Mackenzie, 1993, pp. 21-28).

Most boot camps, contrary to popular belief, are actually located within existing medium- and maximum-security prisons (Mackenzie, 1992). This allows participants to experience the reality of prison thereby increasing the deterrent effects of the program. Administrative goals can also be met by locating the camps within the prisons – both the general inmate population and camp participants can use the same resources and services. Furthermore, it is easier to recruit and replace staff within the prison setting.

The only state that currently operates a "stand-alone" boot camp is New York (Mackenzie, 1992). The state adapted a former wilderness camp to serve its current function. Camp advocates argue that the separate facility does not require expensive high-security equipment, although enhanced programs and staff training are required. The separate camp also allows a more economical use of existing prison space. There are currently eight programs in the United States that are devoted exclusively to dealing with juvenile offenders (Mackenzie, 1993).

Once offenders have completed their terms at boot camp, they are released into the community under supervision. In most states, the offender is released under intensive supervision until he or she is considered a reasonably low security risk. Extensive after-care programs have been implemented in a number of states and were initiated in order to build on the behavioural, social, attitudinal and educational gains the boot camps hope to produce. Three juvenile programs have developed after-care models specifically for boot camps.

These programs offer intensive supervision that includes random urinalysis, curfew checks, employment and other verifications, as well as home visits. Educational classes can also be offered such as General Equivalency Development (GED) preparation and Adult Basic Education (ABE), parenting classes, substance abuse classes, self help groups, family counseling and recreational activities.

The findings from the studies vary considerably based on the evaluation criteria. A study of Florida's program found that the return-to-prison rate for boot camp graduates is 5.59 percent.

Most of the boot camp evaluations conducted have examined the issue of cost savings. A study in Alabama in 1989/90 showed that the cost of housing 153 inmates for ninety days in a boot camp was $550,800 (Burns, 1995, p. 66). The cost to house the same number of inmates in prison for the same period of time was $2,227,680 (Burns, 1995, p. 66). Cost savings only result if boot camp inmates would otherwise have been in regular prison for a longer period.

In Harris County, Texas, an evaluation of the county boot camp measured attitudinal changes in the inmates following boot camp participation (Burton et al., 1994). Ratings were taken to measure attitudes and perceptions of the boot camp staff, of the alcohol and drug counseling, of the AIDS education and counseling, of the boot camp in general, of offenders' future opportunities, of offenders' interpersonal relationships with friends and family and of inmates' self-control, impulsiveness and individual coping skills. In every area except AIDS education and counseling, inmates' attitudes became more positive through the course of the boot camp program. The authors concluded that boot camps have a positive influence on offenders. Further, they noted that other studies that use only recidivism as an indication of success show negative results because there is typically inadequate follow-up care.

Evidence derived from more than a decade, and extensive research evaluating boot camps, led to a proposed framework that boot camps should follow:

- Boot camps should target prison-bound offenders sentenced to relatively lengthy terms of incarceration.
- Participants in boot camps should be selected by correctional officials from incoming prison inmates

to reduce the risk of net-widening (eligibility criteria are often ignored by judges, who tend to use boot camps for low-risk offenders who would not in fact be sent to prison).

- Boot camps should be able to accommodate a large number of offenders.
- In addition to strict discipline and rigorously enforced rules and sanctions for breaches, boot camps should include a high quality rehabilitative component to promote pro-social attitudes and behaviour and minimize in-program rates of failure.
- Rule violators who do not jeopardize public safety or the integrity of the program should be disciplined whenever feasible within the boot camp and in the after-care program rather than re-incarcerated.
- After-care should offer intensive support to facilitate re-integration into society and minimize post-release criminality (Parent, 1995, pp. 146-147).

To date there have been no reported adverse effects on young offenders who have attended correctional boot camps in the United States. Our government should think of this as an investment in our youth – they will be tomorrow's leaders.

This chapter has criticized and addressed a number of topics relating to youth justice. The statistics are very alarming and the question remains: Does our federal government take this responsibility seriously? If they do, why are they not implementing the necessary changes needed to provide a better system for our youth; one that provides the necessary protection and safety for all of us – including them? These children are our future, and the stark reality dictates firm and positive decision-making today. The government has the necessary funding, and they certainly have the power.

Chapter 7 – Provincial and Federal Court Judges

"Mercy to the guilty is cruelty to the innocent."

Adam Smith

"There may be times when we are powerless

to prevent injustice, but there must never

be a time when we fail to protest."

Elie Wiesel

The subject of judges in Canada is a very challenging and complicated issue. They have a tough job, and no one is disputing that. In 2002/03, the adult criminal courts throughout Canada (excluding Manitoba, Northwest Territories and Nunavut) processed 467,500 cases involving approximately 1,042,500 charges, and the mean time elapsed from first to last appearance is often more than six months (*Statistics Canada*). That's a lot of crime, a lot of cases, a lot of delicate decision making.

The justice system works only when appointed judges are reflective and cautious about their tasks and duties. The Canadian people have entrusted them with far-reaching responsibilities that require honour and integrity. The courts are blessed with some undeniably sober judges who have made difficult decisions, and made them well. Canadians are thankful for their efforts in delivering real, honest justice when called upon to do so.

The rest of this chapter, however, will criticize Canada's judges. Judges may be real people who make mistakes, but such mistakes affect the country as a whole. Again and again, judges are making decisions that are ludicrous, dangerous and a slap in the face to victims.

Statistics Canada revealed that in 2002/03, criminals were found guilty in 60 percent of cases heard and 3 percent were acquitted. Thirty-four percent of cases were either stayed, withdrawn, dismissed or discharged, and 3 percent were otherwise terminated by the court (for example, accused found not criminally responsible, found unfit to stand trial, case waived out of province/territory, use of *Charter* arguments). Probation was the most frequently imposed sanction in 46 percent of guilty cases, terms of imprisonment were imposed in 35 percent of cases and a fine was imposed in 33 percent of cases. It seems almost impossible to believe that of all these cases heard, in almost half of the entire caseload, Canadian judges saw fit that a probation sentence was deemed appropriate. Does this mean that half of the criminals found guilty committed very minor crimes? In fact, this seems to suggest that Canada doesn't have a serious crime problem. And it does.

The bench wields a great deal of power. The protection provided to our Canadian judges by the *Provincial Court Act* and the *Judges Act* has made it next to impossible to touch the "untouchables." Accountability for bad decisions is not a part of these Acts. Canada has a number of judges who abuse their power and do what they wish, with little or no consequences. Judges are also failing to implement maximum sentences and are instead letting off violent criminals with probation and short sentences. In 2003, Joe Wamback of the Canadian Crime Victim Foundation said, "It seems judges are in a competition to give the lightest sentence. There is no consequence for violent crime, so there is no justice. Justice statistics from sixty-five countries show Canada is number one when it comes to giving the shortest sentences to criminals." Not something to be proud of.

Some judges feel that federal/provincial legislation is to blame for some of the reasoning behind their decisions. Perhaps if minimum sentences were increased, then judges would be forced to hand down harsher sentences. Apathetic judges should change their attitudes and do whatever they can to make the changes they feel are necessary. Do judges simply not care about the victims, not care about releasing violent criminals, not care that criminals are "getting away with it"? Perhaps their high-end salaries and bloated benefits packages are all they really need; who cares about ethics and virtues?

Or is it more sinister than that? Have some judges been asked to look the other way, do they owe someone a favour, or has money been exchanged? How else can judges explain some of the decisions they've handed down? We have been taught to question what is not logical. Something is seriously wrong with this picture, and the answer needs to be fleshed out.

James Roszko is the perfect example of a judge's bad decision making. In 1993, he was charged with "counseling another person to commit murder" after he offered someone $10,000 to complete the requested task. The charge was dropped after a preliminary hearing, where a judge ruled that "casually talking about killing someone isn't the same as plotting to kill someone."

In September 2001, one of three young men was charged with sexually assaulting a twelve-year-old girl of native origin in Tisdale, Saskatchewan. The four of them drank beer together, and the men took turns having sex with her after picking her up on the steps of a bar. Two of the accused were originally acquitted of the crime, but are now facing another trial after the Appeals Court overturned those verdicts earlier in the year.

The first man charged was found guilty of sexual assault and received a two-year conditional sentence, which he was allowed to serve at home. The Crown prosecutor appealed the lenient sentence on behalf of the girl's family. In April 2005, in Regina, Saskatchewan, the Court of Appeal ruled that this same man should have gone to jail for the crime rather than be allowed to serve his time at home. But the Appeal Court said that locking him up now after he already served nearly his entire two-year sentence at home wouldn't do much good. The three presiding judges wrote, "Even if we were able to set aside the conditional sentencing order, only about four months of his sentence would remain and not all of that would have to be served in prison. Indeed, he would soon qualify for release, so what would that accomplish? Little, if anything."

Justice was definitely not served and decisions like this are an outrage. The cavalier answer delivered by the three Appeal Court judges was shameful. This twelve-year-old girl was a victim of the worst kind, and they call this justice?

In March 2005, in Stonewall, Manitoba, a twenty-two-year-old man from the community of Warren drove drunk and slammed his truck into a group of six teenagers, killing one and seriously injuring another. The presiding judge handed down a sentence of ninety days in jail, followed by three years of supervised probation and a whopping fifty hours of community service labour.

On April 8, 2005, Calgary city police pulled over a vehicle with three suspected top-ranking gang members inside. One of them was wanted on an arrest warrant and all three of them were in violation of court-imposed conditions. Police found several weapons in their search of the vehicle, including a fully loaded Glock pistol with the serial number filed off. The gun was found under a floor mat in a hidden compartment of the vehicle. All three were arrested. Within hours the men were released on bail after appearing before a justice of the peace.

On April 13, 2005, one of the suspected top-ranking gang members was arrested again on a charge of violating an 8:00 p.m. curfew imposed as a condition of his previous release. A provincial court judge refused the Crown's request to revoke his bail, which would have sent him back to jail. A publication ban was then imposed on the submissions at the hearing and the presiding judge's reasons for releasing him.

The reasons for such a decision are flawed: If three people are in a vehicle with a loaded gun, it is difficult to prove who owns the firearm or if the other people in the vehicle knew the gun was there. Shouldn't they all be locked up till one of them fesses up? It's time for judges to set a new precedent in some of these cases.

There have been over twenty-five gang-related incidents on Calgary streets since January, 2005. City police are doing the best possible job they can, but with a shortage of officers and lack of resources, it has become increasingly difficult. Police are also struggling with a justice system that consistently unravels their work in their attempts to control and eliminate the gang violence on our streets. Toronto Police Chief Julian Fantino echoed this sentiment in 2004: "We need a criminal justice system that works more efficiently and effectively to deter people intent on engaging in a life of crime. In today's reality, in the minds of far too many criminals, crime pays. Going to court every couple of days is the price of doing business. Legal aid is provided, they get bail forever, [and] sentences are discounted like bargain basement kinds of sales."

Judges have been given far too much power and there must be a way to control it. Preventative measures must be implemented to ensure that this power is not abused any longer. It would be easy to put simple measures in place to rectify the problems we currently face, if there wasn't so much power wielded by the courts.

To start with, judges should be appointed for very limited terms and subject to public review – not review by other members of the judiciary. The public should have the ability to conduct a review of the judge's overall performance at special intervals, submit their report, and based on the findings of the public review, the judge either stays for another term or not. If judges knew that their careers depended on public scrutiny, justice would return to our courts.

The National Association for Public and Private Accountability (N.A.P.P.A.) has set up a group called the Canada Court Watch Program, operating in Ontario (and attempting to branch out into other provinces). Their main focus begins in the family court system and the goal is to protect the public's interest in the administration of justice in Canada. The Archbishop Dorian A. Baxter, B.A., O.T.C., M. Div. is the National Chairman of the organization and can be contacted through their website, Canada Court Watch Program, at www.canadacourtwatch.com. Canadian judges should review this website and read the "Message to Judges" – it will provide them with some invaluable insight into what Canadians are saying and feeling about our present system of justice in Canada.

On September 9, 2005, "The Canadian Family Forum" published an article by Canadian justice advocate Mike March, who discussed a specific case that took place in June. A thirteen-year-old girl and her family had asked that the media be present at their hearing to protect them from the Children's Aid Society (CAS), the very reason they were at the hearing. Justice Lydia Olah, of Ontario's Superior Court of Justice, ordered the courtroom doors padlocked by Ontario provincial police to prevent the media from participating. This was done without a court order and without arguments being heard by media representatives. The media had the lawful right to be in court and Justice Olah previously threatened members of the media with arrest if they did not get out of her court. What did Justice Olah have to hide, and what was going to be said during the hearing that she refused to let the media hear?

The article also said that some lawyers, speaking from anonymity, have recited cases where they believed court transcripts were altered with the knowledge and consent of judges from Ontario courts in order to cover up wrongdoings by lawyers and judges in the court. These lawyers have reported it would be economic suicide for them to speak publicly about this issue because the judges would make sure that those lawyers paid a heavy price when before the court. One parent from Halton, Ontario, reported that on two occasions, court tapes went missing and were reported lost by the court after he had requested copies of the court transcripts. The parent indicated there were a number of things said by the judge and the opposing lawyer that would have proved embarrassing to both. The court reporter's tape has never been found and likely never will.

The article proposed that maybe the time has come for judges to be elected in Canada so those incompetent and biased judges who bring disrepute to Canada's entire system of justice can be replaced.

All Canadians have a responsibility to make change. If we don't, then we get what we deserve. Working together takes a great deal of patience, effort and understanding, but imagine the rewards: criminals who are actually punished for their crimes, kept off the streets and out of neighbourhoods, and a return to a competently protected society.

Chapter 8 – The Infamous Gun Registry

"$1 Billion to register 7 million guns but only

$8 million to register 40 million cows."

Garry Breitkreuz, Yorkton-Melville, Saskatchewan,

Member of Parliament

"I can honestly say the gun registry is the greatest waste

of law enforcement funds that has ever been

inflicted on the Canadian taxpayer."

Robert H. Head, Retired Assistant Commissioner

Canada's first gun registration requirement was implemented for handguns in 1934. When a permit holder bought a handgun prior to this registration, the person who issued the permit was notified. The new provisions required records identifying the owner, the owner's address and the firearm. Registration certificates were issued and records were kept by the Commissioner of the RCMP or by police departments that provincial Attorneys General had designated as firearms registries. Between 1939 and 1944, re-registration was postponed due to World War II. During the war years, rifles and shotguns had to be registered. This was discontinued after the war ended.

It wasn't until 1968/69 that categories of "firearm," "restricted weapon" and "prohibited weapon" were created for the first time, ending confusion over specific types of weapons and allowing the creation of specific legislative controls for each of the new categories. Bill C-83 was introduced in 1976 proposing new offences and stricter penalties for the criminal misuse of firearms and the prohibition of fully automatic firearms. It also proposed a licensing system requiring anyone aged eighteen or older to get a license to acquire or possess firearms or ammunition.

Bill C-51 passed in the House of Commons in 1977 contained two very big changes: requirements for Firearms Acquisition Certificates (FACs) and requirements for Firearms and Ammunition Business Permits. Fully automatic weapons became classified as prohibited firearms unless they had been registered as restricted weapons before January 1, 1978. Individuals could no longer carry a restricted weapon to protect property and mandatory minimum sentences were re-introduced in the form of a one- to fourteen-year consecutive sentence for the actual use (not mere possession) of a firearm to commit an indictable offence.

Bill C-17 was introduced and enforced between 1991 and 1994. It required a more detailed screening check of FAC applicants. Other major changes included increased penalties for firearm-related crimes, new *Criminal Code* offences, new definitions for prohibited and restricted weapons, new regulations for firearms dealers and clearly defined regulations for the safe storage, handling and transportation of firearms. FAC applicants were required to show knowledge by passing the test for a firearms safety course approved by a provincial Attorney General, or certification by a firearms officer.

After the 1993 federal election, the Liberal Government indicated its intention to proceed with further controls, including some form of licensing and registration system that would apply to all firearms and their owners. A new firearms control scheme and new legislation was drafted, and Bill C-68 was introduced in 1995 with much backlash and criticism from Canadians across the country.

In Canada there are still an estimated 400,000 firearms unlicensed, and by the government's own count, more than 8,000,000 guns remain unregistered. This begs the all-important number one question: Why haven't the Liberals provided Canadians with a reason why? Because they can't.

On March 8, 2005, Garry Breitkreuz, Conservative Member of Parliament for Yorkton-Melville, Saskatchewan, said that the gun registry is going to swallow up another $1.5 million a week to run the program in 2005. Mr. Breitkreuz has become Canada's most well-known anti-gun registry advocate and has since become the Conservative Firearms Critic, after the Liberals rammed the bill through parliament. He also asked that the multi-million dollar registry program be scrapped and the money used to pay for frontline police officers, which the majority of Canadians, 76.6 percent, agreed with according to *JMCK Polling*. He said, "The Auditor General has verified that any value Canadians receive in terms of enhanced safety is miniscule compared to the amount of money being spent."

This is one of the most intelligent comments made by a politician about the gun registry thus far. The billion plus dollars wasted should have been used to provide this country with more police officers and the best equipment and tools. The Liberal Government is incapable of such logical thinking.

On May 13, 2005, Breitkreuz announced that recently released documents show that in the past three years, Canada Custom's Contraband, Intelligence and Investigations has documented and collected fees from more than 251,000 non-residents with firearms traveling in transit or coming into Canada for legal sporting purposes. The documents also show that Canada Border Services Agency does not check to see if these sport shooting tourists and hunters took their guns with them when they left Canada.

This tells Canadians one thing very clearly: The Liberals implemented the section of the *Firearms Act* only to collect the fees for the Canadian Firearms Centre (CFC) but not the section to track the guns. It doesn't really look like the Liberals care about gun control in Canada.

In a recent article from the May, 2005 issue of "Business Report – Western Canada's Conservative Business Voice" regarding the Mayerthorpe tragedy, Mr. Breitkreuz pointed out that the gun registry is essentially useless in protecting police. He cited the following:

- The government does not require that the 176,000 persons prohibited from owning firearms report any change of address to police.

- Police do not track the 37,000 persons with restraining orders against them, or the 12,000 gun owners who have had their firearms licenses refused or revoked.
- The law does not require gun owners to store their registered firearms at their home address or tell the government where they are stored.
- The government does not keep track of registered firearms that are loaned between licensed firearms owners.
- As of August 2004, more than 315,000 handgun owners had failed to re-register more than 600,000 handguns.
- Somewhere between 400,000 and one million gun owners have failed or refused to obtain a firearms license, meaning their guns remain unregistered.
- According to *Statistics Canada* firearm import and export records, the government still has more than ten million guns to register.
- Finally, gun registration certificates contain too few identifying characteristics, making it almost impossible to verify that any particular gun is registered in the system.

The same article commented that the worst part of this entire mess is the very real possibility that the last ten years of the gun registry's prohibitive costs had depleted RCMP resources to the point that a Roszko-type disaster became inevitable. Plus, within the past year, police chiefs such as Toronto's Julian Fantino and Calgary's Jack Beaton have publicly stated that the registry has not helped solve or prevent a single crime, but that it has frequently provided police with inaccurate information.

If the gun registry is such a monumental failure, why do the Liberals continue to defend it? Breitkreuz's answer:

"It's purely political. I've never discovered any other reason. They don't care how much it costs so long as it caters to voters in Quebec, Ottawa, Toronto and Vancouver. Oh, and they love to be thought of as being on the cutting edge of societal development in the United Nations." The Liberals are terrible actors; it's an embarrassment to the citizens of Canada that they continue this phony charade.

With the introduction of Bill C-68 in 1995, James Roszko was required, by legislation, to have a gun license by January 1, 1998. He should also have renewed this license by the year 2003, at the very latest. If Roszko had a gun license, how did he get through the screening process (criminal record checks etc.)? Roszko was banned from owning firearms by the courts in 2000. If he didn't have a license, he shouldn't have been in possession of firearms, and not just firearms, but illegal firearms. He also wasn't charged for these offences under the *Firearms Act*. Once again, the government has failed. They spend money, set up the programs, keep Canadians pacified, and call it a day. The Liberals who supported this ill-conceived gun registry should hang their heads in shame.

This system couldn't even flag a man with a criminal history like Roszko's, a convicted child molester and notorious gun-toting, ill-tempered menace to society. After all, what criminal is going to register his or her guns? Retired Sergeant Randy Nelson, in a letter he sent to the *Edmonton Sun*, said that:

"Roszko was a zero in the system – prohibited from owning firearms. There should not have been so much as a cap on this monster's property...More officers will die amid an ocean of faulty and incomplete firearms data. More civilians will die as a result of misplaced priorities."

Roszko is proof that the gun registry does not aid police officers in any way whatsoever.

The facts are what they are. There's no conspiracy to make Canada's federal government look bad. The Liberal's faulty gun-control legislation may not have caused the deaths of these four wonderful young men, but it certainly played a major role. So did the justice system and parole board, all of which, I might add, the Liberal government is responsible for. Most Canadians continue to feel a deep, wounding sorrow over this tragedy, a sorrow that is finely tempered with rage.

Chapter 9 – Organized Crime in Canada

"There must be a spiritual and moral leadership

rising above economic and political situations.

Governments in both domestic and foreign policies

appeal for popular support by promises of material gain.

We cannot make peace by mere appeal to greed.

We must give the peoples of the world something to live

for as well as something to live on."

John Andres Holmes

"Crime is a fact of the human species, a fact of that

species alone, but it is above all the secret aspect,

impenetrable and hidden. Crime hides, and by far the

most terrifying things are those which elude us."

Georges Bataille

Organized crime in Canada is a disease. It's been around since the early 1900s, and in 1994, nearly one hundred years later, the member states of the United Nations declared this form of crime "public enemy No. 1." Canada's Solicitor General requested an *Angus Reid* poll in 1998 that showed that nine out of ten Canadians considered organized crime a problem. Fifty percent saw it as a very serious one. Seventy-five percent felt that government efforts to fight organized crime should be increased.

Organized crime must be understood in order to recognize how it relates to everything in this book – the lack of funding for RCMP and law enforcement agencies, the politicians, the justice system, correctional services, children, judges and the lawyers. This chapter will explain the links and how everything ties together. Organized crime is a huge industry that has many criminals working for them. The drug dealers, car thieves, smugglers, crystal meth labs and marijuana grow operations are only a few examples of the branches that feed into this extensive food chain. They will do anything to ensure their survival. In order to understand the extent of the problem, Canadians need to be provided with information on how our government has been, is and will be addressing organized crime in Canada.

In 1998, the *Canadian Centre for Justice Statistics* undertook a special study on organized crime in Canada. The information was collected from sixteen major police forces across the country. According to the study, there were five major organized crime groups that are known to operate in Canada:

- Outlaw motorcycle gangs – 24 identified
- Asian-based organized crime groups – 13 identified
- Italian-based organized crime groups – 10 identified

- Aboriginal-based organized crime groups –
  9 identified
- East European-based organized crime groups –
  8 identified

Not surprisingly, the primary characteristics for these groups are the pursuit of profit and power. These groups tend to be assisted by other organized crime groups to facilitate their commission of illegal activities in exchange for goods and services (firearms, personnel, information etc.). Drug trafficking is the most common crime perpetrated by the majority of these organizations. Other common characteristics include having their activities carried out over a prolonged period of time, the use of violence and the commission of serious criminal offences. Asian crime groups tended to concentrate on the trafficking of heroin, while motorcycle gangs were more involved in cocaine and cannabis. The majority of these groups were believed to be heavily involved in money laundering, as well as prostitution and motor vehicle theft.

There were some differences among the five major organized crime groups in terms of their illegal activities outside of drug trafficking. For example, Eastern European groups were found to be more involved in counterfeiting and fraud than other groups; outlaw motorcycle gangs were heavily involved in firearms and explosives trafficking; Asian-based crime groups were more involved in extortion than other groups; Italian-based crime groups were involved in illegal schemes; while Aboriginal crime groups were involved in firearms trafficking.

These criminal organizations maintain relations with one another, which helps to ensure the survival of each organization. They build ties with each other not only to reduce the risk of being caught committing criminal acts, but also to carry on a continuous exchange of goods and services. Violence, intimidation and corruption are effective means of achieving their objectives. These are just some of the risks they are prepared to take in order to ensure their survival and the endless flow of financial gain and power.

The Canadian Security Intelligence Services (CSIS) listed eighteen international criminal organizations in Canada (CSIS, 1998) and the Criminal Intelligence Service Canada (CISC) reported a total of thirty-eight (twenty-four identified) outlaw motorcycle gangs operating throughout the country (CISC, 1998). It is also quite possible that there were additional criminal organizations unknown to authorities at the time.

One half of organized crime groups were believed to exert influence/corruption in the areas of politics, the media, administration, judicial authorities or the economy.

Most large criminal organizations are made up of principal members and associate members – the two differ as to their role within the organization. Motorcycle gangs represent a good example of this distinction. In these gangs, associate members are new prospects. They must be sponsored by one of the principal members of the group – a member who already "wears the colours" (refers to the club's crest and members' most prized possession (RCMP, 1998)). Associates must go through an entire initiation process in which they must prove themselves. Often they have to take on the hardest tasks and the most risky criminal offences. The principal members, for their part, enjoy voting rights, seniority and influence within the group (RCMP, 1994).

Eighty-six percent of criminal organizations were identified by police as being the subject of an investigation during the first seven months of 1998. In the same year, charges were laid against members of almost two-thirds of all identified criminal organizations – 36 percent of all charges were drug-related, 18 percent were for assault and 7 percent were for homicides. According to police, nearly nine in ten organizations (88 percent) were involved in drug trafficking, of which 87 percent were engaged in cocaine trafficking.

Extortion and illegal trafficking in firearms were the next most frequently identified criminal offences, each committed by seven out of ten criminal organizations.

This is the most serious indicator that the gun registry needs to be scrapped. These organizations do not register their guns, and the registry is not stopping them from continuing their activities.

Prostitution is another major activity of these crime groups (63 percent), and it has long been recognized as highly lucrative. Within some of these organizations, prostitution is also considered a means for new immigrants entering Canada illegally to pay their debts to those who enabled them to enter their new country (Adamoli et al., 1998). It is reported that these debts are typically owed for false identification papers (CISC, 1998).

Perhaps this explains some of our many immigration problems and the insurmountable backlog of people in this country who are under deportation orders (by the government's own account). Unfortunately, the government doesn't know where half of them are in order to enforce the orders.

Crimes most frequently committed by organized crime groups are as follows:

- Drug Trafficking – 88 percent
- Firearms (illegal traffic) – 71 percent
- Extortion – 71 percent
- Prostitution – 63 percent
- Vehicle Theft – 60 percent

- Counterfeit/fraud – 56 percent
- Gambling (illegal schemes) – 50 percent

Of all the police forces that responded to this study, money laundering was frequently mentioned. According to the same study, the amount of money laundered in a country can be estimated by calculating 2 percent of its Gross Domestic Product (GDP). This would indicate that the amount of money laundered in Canada was approximately $17 billion (SGC, 1998).

Homicide was identified as the second "other" crime most frequently committed by criminal organizations (7 percent of survey forms). Also identified were assault, smuggling (of immigrants, liquor, cigarettes, consumer goods, jewellery) and fraud (insurance, casino, credit card).

Environmental crimes, including illicit trafficking in endangered species (i.e. bear gallbladders (approx. $15,000 US each), tiger bones, rhino horns) and hazardous wastes (i.e. lead-contaminated waste, PCBs) were identified as having the second greatest impact on Canadian society (after drug trafficking), or more specifically on public health and the environment in general (SGC, 1998). Furthermore, a report issued by British Columbia's Organized Crime Independent Review Committee supports the idea that environmental crime appears to be on the rise in Canada (1998).

As previously mentioned, criminal organizations generally operate within a network – nine crime groups out of ten (93 percent) have been confirmed as having links with other groups. Of these, 85 percent were at the national level and 81 percent at the international level. Other reasons for these groups to maintain links with other crime groups is to use their expertise and skills (58 percent), their personnel (51 percent), and their facilities (43 percent).

Of the five major criminal organizations known to be operating in Canada, it's important for Canadians to know who's doing what, and how they run their operations. There are many similarities but there are also many differences that set them apart.

Outlaw Motorcycle Gangs

More than one-third of criminal organizations identified in Canada were outlaw motorcycle gangs. At present, they are greatly feared because of their highly publicized criminal activities, particularly when they're violent in nature. For example, the Hells Angels received considerable media coverage owing to their war against the Rock Machine for control of the drug trade in Quebec (RCMP, 1998). According to CISC, the Hells Angels are undoubtedly the most feared, powerful and organized of the gangs (CISC, 1998). The one feature of motorcycle gangs that distinguishes them from many other organized crime groups in Canada is their money laundering involvement. Similar to Italian groups, the vast majority of motorcycle gangs identified by respondents were believed to be involved in this activity.

Motorcycle gangs usually have branches in several provinces, known in the organized crime world as "chapters." In 1997, the Hells Angels had 123 chapters throughout the world (RCMP, 1998). The hierarchy in these gangs is based on the tasks performed by each member, and associates (new prospects) within the organization take on the most risky tasks – their role is to protect the principal members (ones who wear the "colours") from the police (RCMP, 1998). It is not unusual for a single gang to have more than a hundred principal and associate members.

These gangs engage in a great variety of criminal activities, the most common of which is drug trafficking, specifically that of cocaine and cannabis. The Hells Angels appear to be heavily involved in the hydroponic cultivation of marijuana; a drug they also export (CISC, 1998). Compared to other criminal organizations in Canada, these gangs are more involved in the illegal trafficking of firearms and explosives. According to the CISC, in October 1997, a major seizure of firearms, grenades and explosives was connected to the well-known war between the Hells Angels and the Rock Machine in Quebec (CISC, 1998).

Extortion and prostitution are other activities these gangs are involved in. Twenty of the twenty-four were believed to be involved in these activities during 1997-98. It is noted that the links between chapters in motorcycle gangs is very strong and links with other criminal organizations are also maintained on both a national and international level – "criminals without borders," as they've been aptly named, are known and feared the world over. At the international level, more than one-third (35 percent) of the links are with criminal organizations in the United States.

Asian-based Organized Crime Groups

Asian-based organized crime groups represent one of the greatest threats in the world of organized crime. They take great care to protect themselves from individuals who may represent a threat or obstacle to their criminal pursuits (Nicaso and Lamothe, 1996). These groups are the second most common identified crime group and are reported to operate on an international scale (twelve out of thirteen surveys) more frequently than other organized crime groups. They are characterized by using legal commercial or business-like structures (i.e. front companies) more frequently than other groups. Another characteristic of these groups is that each person within the organization tends to have specialized tasks.

More than three-quarters of Asian crime groups (ten in thirteen) have more than fifteen associate members. According to the 1998 CISC annual report, a number of Asian crime groups have hundreds of members. For example, some Vietnamese crime groups have 200 to 300 members (CISC, 1998).

Heading up the list in Asian criminal organizations, the most common activities are drug trafficking (mainly opiates and cocaine) and extortion (eleven in thirteen). It appears that these groups dominate the Canadian heroin trade, from importation down to street-level distribution (CISC, 1998).

Police services also identified counterfeiting, illegal smuggling of immigrants and illegal schemes as being frequently perpetrated by these groups (eleven of thirteen). CISC reported that the Asian crime organizations are thought to be responsible for a sizeable trade in counterfeit credit cards – a network that cost Canadian banking institutions $16 million was recently dismantled (CISC, 1998). A favourite sphere of activity in eight of these thirteen identified Asian groups is the illegal smuggling of immigrants that is frequently linked to prostitution. As previously stated, prostitution is often considered a means of payment to the criminal organization who smuggled the person into the country.

Respondents to this study were asked to indicate other criminal activities that these gangs could be associated with. Listed activities included money laundering, credit card fraud, insurance fraud and casino fraud.

Italian-based Organized Crime Groups

Italian-based organized crime groups are undeniably the best known in the organized crime underworld and are primarily associated with the Mafia. Some of them are especially well known in Canada, such as the Cosa Nostra, the Ndrangheta and the Sicilian Mafia – these three are recognized as the most influential (CISC, 1998). These so-called "traditional" crime groups appear to be highly organized and have operated in Canada since the early 1900s. They are usually made up of members of the same family. The Al Capone era of the 1930s and prohibition ushered in a crime wave in Canada (Gomme, 1993).

Similar to the Asian crime groups, Italian criminal groups are distinguished by their frequent use of legal commercial structures (ten out of ten). They have used their sizeable gains from crime to purchase many legitimate businesses and are also involved in money laundering – now identified as one of their priorities (CISC, 1998).

The most common activity is drug trafficking (nine of ten), predominantly that of cocaine. These crime groups have not always been involved in the drug trade (Cretin, 1997); it's only in about the last forty years that they've been involved in such activity (Nicaso and Lamothe, 1996).

Illegal gambling is the next most common criminal activity of Italian crime groups (eight in ten) (CISC, 1998; BC, 1998). Traditional groups operating legitimate businesses such as restaurants often possess illegal gambling machines, etc. (CISC, 1998). Other criminal activities of these groups include extortion (seven in ten) and illegal trafficking in firearms (six in ten). According to all respondents in this study, all of these Italian organizations belong to crime networks – nine of the ten identified maintain links both at the national and international levels. On the international level, five respondents identified the United States as a location of other groups, followed by Italy (four out of nine). For example, the Cuntrera-Caruana clan in Canada is involved in drug trafficking in the province of

Quebec and it maintains links with traditional organizations in Toronto, New York City and Sicily (CISC, 1998).

Aboriginal-based Organized Crime Groups

The origin of Aboriginal-based organized crime is linked to cigarette smuggling. Beare (1996) stated that these crime groups profited from their exemption from taxes and the rise in Canadian cigarette prices compared to cigarette prices in the United States. Since that time, their criminal activities have steadily expanded and diversified (Gomme, 1993).

Geographical factors facilitate illegal activities on the part of Aboriginal groups. For example, the geographic location of reserves in certain provinces lends itself to the trafficking of goods and services. The location of these reserves along the Canada-U.S. border allows for easy cross-border exchange.

These groups are believed to have little involvement in money laundering activities (one in nine). Respondents in this study believe that only two-thirds of aboriginal crime groups commit serious offences, compared to over 91 percent of all other organized crime groups. Aboriginal crime organizations appear to be newcomers to the world of organized crime (Beare, 1996), but respondents (eight of nine) believe they will remain in existence for some time.

Women have a greater presence in these crime groups than in other criminal organizations in Canada – 14 percent were females compared to a 5 percent average in other criminal groups.

The most common criminal activities in these Aboriginal groups are identified as drug trafficking and illegal firearms trafficking (eight of nine). Firearm trafficking has only recently become an increased priority for authorities because of its growth.

According to the study, robbery, prostitution and motor vehicle theft are also perpetrated by two-thirds of these crime groups. Liquor and tobacco smuggling was specifically mentioned as one of the involved activities, activities more commonly found on reserves in Quebec (CISC, 1998; BC, 1998).

All Aboriginal crime groups maintain links at the national level. These few links are usually in the United States and are related to the theft of motor vehicles and smuggling.

Eastern European-based Organized Crime Groups

Some of the respondents in this study feel that Eastern-based crime groups will be the next wave in the world of organized crime (RCMP, 1998; Nicaso and Lamothe, 1996). However, these organizations have existed for hundreds of years with organized crime groups in Russia and Eastern Europe since the seventeenth century (CSIS, 1998). Eight of the survey questionnaires identified these groups as being operative in Canada.

According to the study, Eastern European organized crime groups exert less discipline and control over their members (four of eight) compared to 95 percent of all other criminal groups. Further, these groups are less prone to using violence or other means of intimidation than other criminal groups (two of eight).

In Russia alone there are between 5000 and 8000 criminal organizations, and together they have approximately 100,000 members (CSIS, 1998). In Canada, however, it appears they have much smaller memberships. The most favoured illegal activities by these groups are counterfeiting (heavily involved) and motor vehicle theft. It appears that one of the preferred activities of these organizations is the smuggling of consumer goods, usually motor vehicles destined for Eastern Europe (CISC, 1998).

Drug trafficking, prostitution and extortion are also common activities. Following the dismantling of the Soviet Union, Russian criminal organizations expanded their illegal activities on the international scene. These new "criminals without borders" threaten to introduce a new form of smuggling into the crime world – namely the smuggling of radioactive materials (Nicaso and Lamothe, 1996).

Six of eight of these identified crime groups in Canada are known to maintain links with other organizations – of these, three maintain links at the national level. Five of these six organizations maintain links with other organized groups at the international level, mainly in Russia and the United States. These links are an advanced indicator of increasingly sophisticated activities on the part of Eastern European organizations in Canada (CISC, 1998).

These statistics show the problems organized crime presents to Canada. As stated, the corruption of politics, the media, public administration, judicial authorities or the economy is a mitigating factor and of huge concern, considering that over half of organized crime groups in this country are involved in this corruption. In order to continue penetrating and dismantling organized crime, the federal government must make this a priority by providing the necessary funding and resources to assist in winning the battle or gaining control. If the government does not put substantially needed funding and effort into addressing the issues, then we have to question why. Government negligence allows organized crime to ultimately gain control over our nation.

Chapter 10 – The Lawyers

"To educate a man in mind and not in morals is

to educate a menace to society."

Theodore Roosevelt

"Those who use the law as shoemakers use leather;

rubbing it, pressing it, and stretching it with their teeth,

all to the end of making it fit their purposes."

Louis XII

Everyone is entitled to fair representation under the law. Problems arise when making money or building a reputation overshadows a client's guilt or innocence.

Guy Fontaine, Roszko's lawyer for more than fifteen years, said that his client underwent a psychiatric assessment at Alberta Hospital in Edmonton on one occasion and was given a "clean bill of health." Fontaine admitted, though, to being a little afraid of his client and that he was never one to be messed with: "He was very self-righteous. He was always right, and everyone was out of line. There was no love lost between Roszko and the RCMP." He knew that his client was a ticking time bomb with a short fuse. Fontaine gave a number of negative media interviews without much hesitation after the tragedy. This kind of attitude and hypocrisy in the legal profession leaves a bad taste in an honest person's mouth. If Fontaine was so concerned about his client's self-righteous attitude and hatred for police, then why didn't he decline to defend his client?

Peter Wilson is another lawyer defending a guilty client and working tirelessly to appeal a second-degree murder conviction and life sentence. His client is Kelly Ellard, who mercilessly beat and drowned a young girl in 1997. Reena Virk was lured to a bridge in Victoria by a group of teenagers and died a horrible death. A witness in the case testified that after beating her severely, Ellard dragged her to the water and held her head underneath until she drowned.

Mr. Wilson is seeking either an acquittal or a fourth trial. Yes, a fourth trial. He has filed documents to the court briefly outlining the grounds for an appeal of her conviction and sentence. It seems Ms. Ellard's lawyer thought the imposed sentence was excessive.

Give me a break. She's been found guilty of second-degree murder after beating a young girl unconscious and drowning her. An automatic life sentence is, I believe, a very just and deserving sentence.

The Canadian public is sick of these self-righteous lawyers. They must stop abusing the *Canadian Charter of Rights and Freedoms* to free the guilty, stop turning the Charter and Canadian Constitution into a circus ring, stop using ridiculous technicalities to ban or throw out concrete evidence.

Public defenders and some of the high-powered and wealthy criminal law lawyers in this country should look at the evidence presented, defend their client based on the evidence (or lack thereof) and accept the outcome. The old adage of "let the evidence speak for itself" doesn't seem to apply any more. Defending criminals has become a multi-billion dollar growth industry, and it's not because criminals are innocent. The abuse is absolute.

What is really tough to swallow is that the majority of defending criminal lawyers are very much aware of their client's guilt – plea bargaining is proof of that. It makes no difference to them that their client murdered the father of three small children, raped and brutally beat some poor woman, robbed a liquor store and shot the clerk. The only thing that matters to them is their sleazy reputation, the power obtained from their accomplishment in manipulating the system and the dollars that feed their bank account.

Lawyers who prosecute criminals or the defenders of the truly innocent are given a bad name because of the slime that happens to be lumped in the same profession. Thankfully, there are lawyers out there who can tolerate this ugliness and still continue to take the needs of victims seriously in order to see that justice is served. They should be commended for their hard work and compassion. This country needs more lawyers of this high calibre, who are morally and ethically responsible.

Chapter 11 – The Time for Change is Now

"I am a Canadian, free to speak without fear,

free to worship in my own way, free to stand for

what I think right, free to oppose what I believe wrong,

or free to choose those who shall govern this country.

This heritage of freedom I pledge to uphold

for myself and all mankind."

John Diefenbaker

(From the Canadian Bill of Rights, July 1, 1960)

On Tuesday, June 28, 2005, the families of slain RCMP Constables Leo Johnston, Anthony Gordon, Peter Schiemann and Brock Myrol came together and stood proudly in Calgary, Alberta, to launch a pin campaign honouring our four lost Mounties. The commemorative pin bears the image of four RCMP Stetsons with an officer sitting proudly on his horse, a symbol of their strength and determination. Emblazoned on the pin are the words "WE REMEMBER 2005."

These four families are intent on putting much needed pressure on the federal government. They are calling for much harsher sentences and increased funding for law enforcement to fight the war on crime. They will be taking their fight to Ottawa this fall.

Reverend Don Schiemann said that failing to change laws would insult the memories of his son, Peter, and the three other officers. He added, "if we ignore these issues and choose to forget, I will no longer be able to wear this pin proudly. We need to take a hard, long look at our justice system that would allow a person like Roszko...out on parole so he could carry out his plan to kill those officers." An emotional Reverend Schiemann continued, "if repeat, dangerous offenders are not held more accountable, there could be a time bomb waiting to go off, and next time it could be more than four officers." He called for a national non-partisan debate surrounding the deaths of the four boys that would include the wisdom of providing more resources to the RCMP.

Keith Myrol, father of slain Constable Brock Myrol, told the *Calgary Herald*, "there's one thing I used to say and I don't say it anymore. For years, somebody would be complaining about some little thing and I would always say, 'Canada is a great nation, at least we don't have to worry about people shooting at us.' You know what? Now we do. So I don't say it anymore and now I want it to stop.

Brock joined the RCMP to make a difference, and you know what? He is going to."

Any nation that cares about the endless efforts of law enforcement and the people who take on that task on our behalf, must take a long, hard look in the mirror after a tragedy such as this.

It is time to honour our fallen heroes by ensuring that the law enforcement community in Canada has the protection and resources it needs to operate safely and effectively. Above all else, we must try to ensure that we don't suffer any more loss than we already have. With my entire heart and soul, I proudly ask every single decent, honest, hardworking Canadian to remember to do what's right instead of what they think is politically correct. There comes a time when we have to look in the mirror and do the right thing in the name of justice for all of us who have lost someone they love because of a violent act of crime. It doesn't matter whether the person they loved was a police officer or an innocent bystander who just happened to be caught in the crossfire. This is one commonality we all share, and we've all been affected by some kind of tragedy just like this one. These tragic moments in our lives often happen because our justice system has failed us miserably.

We must ask ourselves how we can allow this to continue to happen. It is time for a changing of the guard. One that will take our needs, the protection of our children, safety, security and right to freedom that we have fought so bravely for – and take it seriously. It is time for our government to listen, and listen carefully. We, as Canadians, have the power to put into place those who will see that proper and just changes are made within a system that is so inadequate that it boggles the mind and causes us to lose sleep at night.

Many Canadians will respond to this book with accusations that I have it in for the Liberal Government – I have it in for no one. I am relying on history and facts. It doesn't matter which political party wields the power, what matters is that Canadians are suffering and paying a very dear price for the way this country is being horribly mismanaged.

Something good must come of this. The way I see it, we will either have a new government that will take Canadians' wants, needs and wishes seriously; or we'll have an existing government that will, in short order, become accountable to Canadians and realize that our voices will dictate the former or the latter. Either way, the citizens of Canada will win. Our four young Mounties would be proud of that.

The loss these families have suffered and the issues surrounding it isn't so much about James Roszko, it's about doing everything in their power to at least try and prevent this from happening again. These deaths could have been prevented, and it's up to our government to provide the necessary changes toward that goal. An ounce of prevention was all that was needed. Mahatma Gandhi once said, "We must become the change we want to see."

As Canadians we have much to be proud of. The *Canadian Charter of Rights and Freedoms* is one of those things. It is the foundation of the ground that we walk on and the grass beneath our feet. Throughout my research for this book, it came to light that many Canadians have never actually read the Charter – it is something that every Canadian should do at least once. For those of you who have not read it, take the time to do so, be proud of who you are and celebrate that thought. For those of you who have read it, please read it again and think about the foundation it was built upon and where we are today. For those of you in the name of "injustice" who have abused, twisted, warped and demeaned it in order to protect those who have murdered, maimed, killed, raped, abused or harmed any person or child in this country, I have only this to say: "There, but for the grace of God, go I."

This may not be the end. This may be the beginning of many things yet to come. My hopes, wishes and prayers for each of the grieving families will always be in my heart. I believe Canada still grieves with each and every one of you, and I hope that all our efforts together will finally bring you some peace of mind.

Something good will come of this tragedy – it has to.

I very clearly remember the solitary bugler, who stood with a haunting, yet visible pride in his Red Serge and felt Stetson as he sounded "The Last Post" – it signified the end of the memorial service at the Butterdome in Edmonton, Alberta, on March 10, 2005.

As for myself, "The Last Post" came to have a completely different meaning – it signified not the end, but the beginning of what I can only hope will be the coming changes this country is in such desperate need of.

In honour of Brock, Leo, Anthony and Peter.

As promised, your letters of support for much needed change and comments can be mailed or sent to the following:

The Last Post

PO Box 51149
8120 Beddington Blvd. NW
Calgary, AB T3K 3V9

thelastpost@telus.net

The Prime Minister of Canada

The Right Honourable Paul Martin
Prime Minister of Canada
Office of the Prime Minister
80 Wellington Street
Ottawa, ON, Canada K1A 0A2

Anne McLellan, Deputy Prime Minister & Minister of Public Safety and Emergency Preparedness

Postage Free to:
Minister's Office
Department of Public Safety and
    Emergency Preparedness
340 Laurier Avenue W.
Sir Wilfred Laurier Building, 13th Floor
Ottawa, ON, Canada K1A 0P8

Provincial Premiers of Canada

The Honourable Ralph Klein
Premier of Alberta
307 Legislature Bldg.
10800 – 97 Avenue
Edmonton, AB, Canada T5K 2B6

The Honourable Gordon Campbell
Premier of British Columbia
Box 9041
Station PROV GOVT
Victoria, BC, Canada V8W 9E1

The Honourable Gary Doer
Premier of Manitoba
Legislative Assembly of Manitoba
450 Broadway
Winnipeg, MB, Canada R3C 0V8

The Honourable Bernard Lord
Premier of New Brunswick
Box 6000
Fredericton, NB, Canada E3B 5H1

The Honourable Danny Williams
Premier of Newfoundland and Labrador
Confederation Building, East Block
Box 8700
St John's, NL, Canada A1B 4J6

The Honourable Joseph Handley
Premier of the Northwest Territories
Legislative Assembly of the Northwest Territories
Box 1320
Yellowknife, NT, Canada X1A 2L9

The Honourable John Hamm
Premier of Nova Scotia
One Government Place
7th Floor, 1645 Granville St
PO Box 726
Halifax, NS, Canada B3J 2T3

The Honourable Paul Okalik
Premier of Nunavut
P.O. Box 1200
Iqaluit, Nunavut, Canada X0A 0H0

The Honourable Dalton McGuinty
Premier of Ontario
Legislative Building
Queen's Park
Toronto, ON, Canada M7A 1A1

The Honourable Patrick Binns
Premier of Prince Edward Island
Fifth Floor South, Shaw Building
95 Rochford Street
P.O. Box 2000
Charlottetown, PEI, Canada C1A 7N8

The Honourable Jean Charest
Premier of Quebec
Édifice Honoré-Mercier
835, boul. René-Lévesque Est 3e étage
Quebec, Quebec, Canada G1A 1B4

The Honourable Lorne Calvert
Premier of Saskatchewan
Room 226, Legislative Building
Regina, SK, Canada S4S 0B3

The Honourable Dennis Fentie
Premier of the Yukon
Box 2703
Whitehorse, Yukon, Canada Y1A 2C6

Source Information Resources
and Document References

Statistics Canada:

Statistics Canada information is used with the permission of the Minister of Industry, as Minister responsible for Statistics Canada. Information on the availability of the wide range of data from Statistics Canada can be obtained from Statistics Canada's Regional Offices, its World Wide Web Site at http://www.statcan.ca, and its toll-free access number 1-800-263-1136.

Chapter 1

1. Source: The Edmonton Journal – "Assault rifle eluded three police searches: Roszko believed to have brought weapon from U.S. 25 years ago," March 9, 2005, Page A3.

2. Source: CTV.ca website, "The Shooter", www.ctv.ca/generic/WebSpecials/rcmp/shooter.html.

Chapter 2

1. Source: Clancy of the Mounted Police by Robert William Service (first paragraph), www.geocities.com/Heartland/Bluffs/8336/ robertservice/clancy.html

2. Source: The Calgary Sun – "Vests no protection against rifle," March 7, 2005, Page 4.

3. Source: The Calgary Herald – "Killer stalked Mounties in campaign of terror: Roszko followed officers' wives around town," March 8, 2005, Page A1/Front.

4. Source: The Calgary Sun – "The Fallen Four – Our Thoughts Are With You," March 10, 2005, Page 28.

5. Source: RCMP Media Briefing – Alberta – "Shooting death of Four Mayerthorp/Whitecourt RCMP Members – March 3, 2005," March 21, 2005.

6. Source: The Calgary Sun – "Cops short armour cash," March 26, 2005, Page 3.

7. Source: They Are Our Heroes. We Shall Not Forget Them, http://cacp.ca/english/memoriam/ results.asp?alphabetletter=B, April 4, 2005.

8. Source: 38th Parliament, 1st Session – Edited Hansard, Number 032, November 25, 2004.

9. Source: Excerpts, adapted from Statistics Canada publication, "Police resources in Canada", 2002-2003, Catalogue 85-225, December 16, 2004, page 13.

Chapter 3

1. Source: www.gov.ab.ca/acn/200504/178592F6D2682-F425-443C-8E0115064A926A3F.html, April 15, 2005, "Solicitor General reaffirms commitment to policing in Calgary".

2. Source: The Calgary Sun – "Politicians shocked," March 4, 2005, Page 29.

3. Source: The Calgary Sun – "Political furor sparked," March 5, 2005, Page 22.

4. Source: The Calgary Herald – "Promises kept, says Martin," March 5, 2005, Page A10.

5. Source: Red Deer Advocate – "City grieves," March 7, 2005.

6. Source: The Calgary Sun – "Civil servants hit the jackpot," June 3, 2005, Page 7.

Chapter 4

1. Source: Canada's System of Justice, www.canada.justice.gc.ca/en/dept/pub/just/01.html, Department of Justice, 2005. Reproduced with the permission of the Minister of Public Works and Government Services Canada, 2005.

2. Source: www.gov.ab.ca/acn/200504/17860F25B119B-4A2D-4535-97653C404455ECBA.html, April 16, 2005, "Access to justice system will be better, easier".

3. Source: Excerpts, adapted from the Statistics Canada publication "The Daily", Impaired driving and other traffic offences, November 7, 2003

4. Source: Excerpts, adapted from the Statistics Canada publication "Juristat", Catalogue No. 85-002, Vol. 22, No. 11, October 31, 2002, pages 1-3 and 5-11.

5. Source: www.addiction-rehab.info/ methamphetamine-addiction.html, "Methamphetamine Addiction," September 30, 2005.

6. Source: Excerpts, adapted from the Statistics Canada publication "Juristat", Catalogue No. 85-002, Vol. 20, No. 12, December 4, 2000, pages 1, 3-5, and 7-10.

7. Source: Excerpts, adapted from the Statistics Canada publication "Juristat", Catalogue 85-002, Vol. 24, No. 1, February 23, 2004, pages 1, 2, 5, 7, 8, 10 and 11.

8. Source: Auditor General's Report, Chapter 4, 2002, http://64.233.167.104/search?q=cache:YRSN_cxot CgJ:www.oag-bvg.gc.ca/domino/media..., The Criminal Justice System: Significant Challenges.

9. Source: The Calgary Sun, Letters to the Editor – "Country is full of contradictions," August 14, 2005.

Chapter 5

1. Source: http://www.slais.ubc.ca/courses/libr500/00-01-wt2/www/J_Haines/crimes1.htm, Sex Offenders Registries – "Christopher Stephenson," September 27, 2005.

2. Source: Edmonton Police Service, News Release – Public information and warning, November 22, 2002.

3. Source: The Calgary Sun – "Tracking plan called big joke," March 20, 2005, page 12.

4. Source: The Calgary Sun – "Abuser faces restrictions," April 21, 2005, Page 3.

5. Source: Excerpts, adapted from the Statistics Canada publication "Adult correctional services in Canada (data tables)", 2002-2003, Catalogue No. 85-211, October 27, 2004, Pages 7-9.

6. © Source: www.csc-scc.gc.ca/text/programs_e.shtml, Correctional Services of Canada. Reproduced with the permission of the Minister of Public Works and Governmental Services Canada, 2005.

7. Source: Dept. of Justice *Basic Principles of Justice for Victims of Crime text, Justice Canada Web Site*, Dept. of Justice Canada. Reproduced with the permission of the Minister of Public Works and Government Services, 2005.

8. Source: Excerpts, adapted from the Statistics Canada publication "Victim services in Canada: national, provincial and territorial fact sheets", 2002-2003, Catalogue 85-003, December 9, 2004, pages 6-8.

9. Source: Excerpts, adapted from the Statistics Canada publication "Restorative justice programs and services in criminal matters: Summary of consultations", 2002-2003,Catalogue 85-562, December 11, 2003, pages 7-11, 16, 31 and 32.

10. Source: www.gov.ab.ca/acn/200506/ 1813282FB5A1D-7C5F-4D9F-B4EA9F338D311016.html, June 2, 2005, "Funding for victim services reaches all time high".

11. Source: The Calgary Sun – "Prisoner's game-play suffering in remand," April 6, 2005.

12. Source: The Calgary Sun – "Remand beating alleged," – April 8, 2005.

13. Source: The Calgary Sun – "Apology for perv," April 13, 2005, Page 24.

14. Source: The Calgary Sun – "Feds fund prisoners' leave," July 20, 2005, Page 3.

15. Source: The Calgary Sun – "MP calling for inmate travel price tag," July 21, 2005, Page 18.

16. Source: www.mcso.org/index.asp, Maricopa County Sheriff's Office website, July 25, 2005.

17. Source: Excerpts, adapted from the Statistics Canada publication, "A one-day snapshot of inmates in Canada's adult correctional facilities", Catalogue 85-601, No. 1, March 17, 1999, pages 325-329, 334 and 336.

18. Source: Excerpts, adapted from the Statistics Canada publication, "Graphical overview of the criminal justice indicators", 2000-2001, Catalogue 85-227, November 5, 2002, pages 56, 60 and 62.

19. Source: www.johnhoward.ab.ca/PUB/
    respaper/privpr02.htm, "Private Prisons",
    John Howard Society of Alberta, 2002,
    pages 1-6, 9-11, 13 and 15.

20. Source: www.johnhoward.ab.ca/docs/UserFees/
    htm, "Correctional User Fees", John Howard
    Society of Alberta, 2001, pages 1, 3 and 6.

Chapter 6

1. Source: Excerpts, adapted from the Statistics
    Canada publication "Family violence in Canada: a
    statistical profile 2004", Catalogue 85-224,
    July 6, 2004, pages 1-3, 21 and 39.

2. Source: Excerpts, adapted from the Statistics
    Canada publication "Canadian crime statistics",
    2003, Catalogue 85-205, October 13, 2004,
    pages 11-12.

3. Source: www.johnhoward.ab.ca/PUB/C8.htm,
    John Howard Society of Alberta, *Alternative
    Custody Programs For Youth, 1997.*

4. Source: www.johnhoward.ab.ca/PUB/C34.htm,
    John Howard Society of Alberta, *Boot Camps: Issues
    For Canada, John Howard Society of Alberta, 1998.*

5. Source: http://sympaticomsn.ctv.ca/servlet/
    ArticleNews/story, CTVNews/
    20050816_taber_shooter_050816?hub=topstories.
    "Taber shooter back in police custody,"
    August 17, 2005.

6. Source: The Calgary Sun – "Victim slams
    sentence," June 3, 2005, Page 10.

Chapter 7

1. Source: www.ctv.ca/generic/WebSpecials/rcmp/ shooter.html, "The Shooter".

2. Source: The Calgary Sun – "Bail decision riles police," April 12, 2005, Page 3.

3. Source: The Calgary Sun – "Suspected gang member granted bail," April 22, 2005.

4. Source: The Calgary Sun – "No jail in sexual assault of girl," April 21, 2005, Page 24.

5. Source: Excerpts, adapted from the Statistics Canada publication, "Juristat", Catalogue No. 85-002, Vol. 20, No. 12, November 27, 2003, page 1.

6. Source: www.canadacourtwatch.com website, Court Watch Home Page, PDF, "Canadians are getting wise to the lies and corruption of Canada's broken family and domestic violence Courts", September 9, 2005.

Chapter 8

1. Source: The Calgary Herald – "RCMP murders spark questions about gun registry," March 8, 2005, Page A6.

2. Source: www.cfc.gc.ca/pol-leg/hist/ firearms/firearms_control_e.asp, Canada Firearms Centre website, "History of Firearms Control in Canada: Up to and Including the Firearms Act," September 29, 2005.

3. Source: www.garrybreitkreuz.com/ breitkreuzgpress/2005_May_13.htm, *Firearms Centre Shortchanges Border Agency.*

4. Source: www.garrybreitkreuz.com/ breitkreuzgpress/2005_June_17.htm, *$1 Billion to Register 7 Millions Guns But Only $8 Million to Register 40 Million Cows.*

5. Source:http://66.102.7.104/search?q=cache: vIT1Sa8XB3kJ:www.garrybreitkreuz.com/ publications/, "What Police Have Said About The Gun Registry," by Garry Breitkreuz, MP – Updated: July 5, 2005.

6. Source: Business Report – Western Canada's Conservative Business Voice, "The Gun Registry's Deadliest Day," May 2005 Issue.

Chapter 9

1. Source: Excerpts, adapted from the Statistics Canada publication "Organized crime activity in Canada: a pilot survey of 16 police services", Catalogue 85-548, No. 1, May 20, 1999, pages 4, 7, 8, 12 and 14-27.

2. Source: www.ecobridge.org/contents/s_ill.htm, "Illegal Trade in Wildlife and Wildlife Products, September 29, 2005.

Chapter 10

1. Source: The Calgary Sun – "Lawyer recalls long history of clashes with the law," March 4, 2005, Page 4.

Chapter 11

1. Source: The Calgary Herald – "RCMP ambush 'a wake-up call': Justice system must change, slain Mounties' Families demand," June 28, 2005, Page A1/Front.

The Last Post

**Tragedy in Alberta: How the Deaths of Four Alberta RCMP
Officers Will Not Be Forgotten**

Order Form

To order additional copies of The Last Post for
yourself, or a friend, please complete the form below.
And remember, $1.00 from every copy sold goes to
the "Always Remembered Memorial Fund"
established for the families of the slain officers.

The Last Post _____x $ 15.95   = $_____

Postage and Handling @ 5.00 per copy   = $_____

Subtotal   = $_____

In Canada add 7% GST   = $_____

Total enclosed   = $_____

Name: _____

Address: _____

City: _____   Province: _____

Postal Code: _____   Email: _____

Please mail your order and payment to:

The Last Post

PO Box 51149
8120 Beddington Blvd. NW
Calgary, AB T3K 3V9

WE REMEMBER MEMORIAL PINS

On March 3rd, 2005, our nation was united in sadness when
Royal Canadian Mounted Police Constables
Anthony Gordon, Leo Johnston, Brock Myrol & Peter Schiemann
tragically lost their lives in service to their country
while carrying out their duties near Mayerthorpe, Alberta.

Wear a pin. Show We Remember.

Name: _____

Address: _____

Town/City: _____ Prov: _____

Phone: _____ Postal Code: _____

Pins sell for $5.00 each, GST incl.

Order Form		
No. of Pins	**$5.00 per pin**	**Total**
	X $5.00	=
Shipping & Handling 1-5 pins - $1 • 6-10 pins - $2 • 11-15 pins - $3 *for orders more than 15 pins, please add $1 for each additional 1-5 pins GST is included*	+ =	

Method of Payment:	Cheques/Money Orders can
☐ Cheque ☐ Credit Card	be made out to: **RCMP In Trust Always Remembered Fund**

Credit Card Information   Name on Card

☐ MasterCard ☐ Visa   _____

Card No. _____ Exp. Date ____/____

Please send your completed order form and payment to:
RCMP Veterans Assoc. Edmonton
Attn: RCMP Always Remembered Fund
11140 109 Street
Edmonton, AB
T5G 2T4

Thank you